Books by Benjamin Appel
WHY THE RUSSIANS ARE THE WAY THEY ARE
WHY THE CHINESE ARE THE WAY THEY ARE
WHY THE JAPANESE ARE THE WAY THEY ARE

# Why the Japanese Are
# the Way They Are

# Why the Japanese Are the Way They Are

by Benjamin Appel

LITTLE, BROWN AND COMPANY
BOSTON    TORONTO

FIRST EDITION

T 03/73

Library of Congress Cataloging in Publication Data

Appel, Benjamin, 1907-
    Why the Japanese are the way they are.

    Bibliography: p.
    1. Japan--History. 2. National characteristics,
Japanese. I. Title.
DS835.A7            915.2'03          72-1806
ISBN 0-316-048666

915.2
AP 48 w

*Published simultaneously in Canada
by Little, Brown & Company (Canada) Limited*

PRINTED IN THE UNITED STATES OF AMERICA

APR 12 1973 PUB.

CY 111

32

# Contents

# Maps

# Why the Japanese Are
# the Way They Are

# ONE

# Great Leap to the West

THE FIRST WHITE MEN to visit Japan, the Portuguese, came in 1542 seeking the fabulous treasure described by Marco Polo, the Venetian. Marco Polo had served seventeen years — from 1275 to 1292 — at the court of Kublai Khan, the Mongol emperor of China. The Khan's fleets in 1274 and again in 1281 had failed in their attempts to invade and seize the riches of the little kingdom in the sea. Marco Polo would record these events in his book of travels. His tales of the Orient, like a second *Thousand and One Nights,* inflamed the imagination of all Europe.

To the Japanese, the Portuguese were "barbarians" — a strange race who practiced a strange religion and carried strange weapons. Christianity, symbolized by the cross, intrigued the Japanese, many of whom would become converts. The firearms from across the seas astonished a people who knew only the sword and the bow.

"The article was used in this way," a Japanese eyewitness commented on the Portuguese arquebus or light handgun. "Some mysterious medicine was put into it with a small round piece of lead, and when one lit the medicine . . . the lead piece was discharged and hit everything."

Japanese metalworkers studied "the article" until they had mastered its principles sufficiently to make the first Japanese arquebus. It was an omen of things to come. For in a distant and utterly unimaginable century, Japanese mechanics would produce artillery and battleships. Japanese military forces in the Russo-Japanese War of 1904–1905 would defeat the Russian armies and scuttle the Russian navies. And still later in that same century of wars and revolutions, Japanese aerial armadas would strike a mighty blow at the United States on December 7, 1941.

All these events were in the incalculable future.

The Portuguese explorers were followed by Spaniards, Dutchmen, Britishers. All bowed their heads to the Prince of Peace even as they fought each other for trading privileges. In their hearts they all — as the Japanese shoguns, or military leaders, suspected — hoped to subvert the Island Empire.

The quarrels and plots of the traders, the activities

and successes of the missionaries, alarmed the Japanese authorities. Christianity was declared to be an illegal religion and the "barbarians," whether they dealt in silk or in the souls of men, were expelled. The Dutch alone remained, confined to a single trading station. Once a year a Dutch ship sailed from the Chinese mainland to the island of Kyushu. No other Western ship could trade or even anchor in a Japanese port.

Century after century, the Japanese islands were as isolated from the West as if on another planet.

Across the Pacific, a young American nation had initiated a profitable trade with ancient China. American clipper ships, carrying furs from the Pacific northwest, regularly sailed to Canton where a pelt that cost fourteen cents would fetch as much as a hundred dollars. In 1791, two American ships bound for Canton stopped at a Japanese port to sell sea-otter skins. Their welcome was icy and they quickly hoisted anchor. Year after year, still other traders continued to knock, if without success, on "the closed door." They complained to their representatives in Washington, D.C., who responded with pious speeches. Wasn't it America's God-given duty to lead the Oriental peoples into an age of progress? U.S. Senator Thomas Hart Benton of Missouri expressed the belief that the white race should, "wake up and reanimate the torpid body of Asia."

The first white men in Japan had been armed with

arquebuses. The guns were far more formidable when Commodore Matthew C. Perry's squadron of four "black ships" — as the Japanese called them — entered the Japanese port of Uraga in 1853. The loaded cannon on Perry's ships were never fired but they backed up the American demand for a trade treaty.

The Japanese rulers, the shogun and his nobles, feared the war-making abilities of the West. The Dutch trading station, small as it was, had been their post office to the world. Japanese scholars had studied the Dutch language in the seventeenth century in order to read the Dutch medical works. Medicine was the only Western science that had been permitted to "enter" Japan. Nevertheless, the shoguns and the emperor had been kept informed of the many other sciences flourishing beyond the seas, including the deadly science of warfare.

In February, 1854, Perry returned from the China coast with a squadron of nine ships. He asked what the decision had been regarding a trade treaty. Again, no cannon were fired but this time "the closed door" was unlocked. Perry got his trade treaty. Soon afterwards the other trade-hungry Western nations, including Tsarist Russia, were granted similar privileges.

No formal treaty, however, could dissolve the long centuries of isolation. Hatred for the "barbarians" erupted in a series of ugly incidents that reached a climax in 1863 when a group of samurai or warriors set fire to the British legation. That same year the shogun expelled the "barbarians." But this situation didn't continue.

The guns had become too powerful. A Western fleet shelled the coastal towns and in the roar of cannon the nation finally awoke from its long feudal sleep.

The wind of change swept away the past and the men of the past: the succession of shoguns or absolute military rulers who in the name of the emperor had governed Japan for almost seven centuries. The title shogun was first held by Yoritomo, a military genius, in the year 1192. He was succeeded by members of his family, the Minamato clan who exercised supreme power for a hundred and fifty years.

There were weak shogunates and powerful shogunates. From 1603 to 1867, the Tokugawa family, like some hereditary dictatorship, ruled Japan. Threatened by the superior power of the West, the fifteenth Tokugawa shogun resigned in 1867. One year later, in 1868, the entire nation turned to the Emperor Meiji for guidance.

To the Japanese, their emperors were semidivine figures, the Kings of Heaven, earthly descendants of the Goddess of the Sun. Meiji, like all his predecessors, was a living symbol of continuity. The Tokugawas and other powerful families or clans before them had overshadowed innumerable emperors — but no shogun had ever disputed the ultimate authority of the Kings of Heaven. The sun, too, was often hidden by clouds but inevitably the clouds vanished and the sun again blazed in regal splendor.

Emperor Meiji, 1852–1912, was only eighteen when he ascended the imperial throne in 1868. That same year he issued a new law which declared: "The absurd customs and practices of the past should be discarded and justice should be based on the laws of heaven and earth. . . . Wisdom shall be sought all over the world in order to establish firmly the foundations of the empire."

Meiji, emperor and reformer, personally set an example for his subjects. By eating beef, he violated the Buddhist religious precepts that had endured a thousand years. Buddhism forbade the slaughter of animals. Century after century, people had lived on fish in all their variety, and on rice and vegetables. Meat, bloody meat, was deemed unfit for human beings. By dining on beefsteak Meiji demonstrated that it was now perfectly respectable to eat the flesh of a "four-legged animal."

If beef represented Western progress, so did short hair. Japanese men had always worn their hair long — Meiji had his hair cropped. It was more difficult to convince his officers to give up their long medieval swords. The sword was "the soul of the samurai." When the imperial suggestions continued to be resisted, Meiji issued an order in 1886 that could not be disobeyed. During his long reign of forty-four years Japan acquired more and more Western customs. Japanese missions like eager schoolboys traveled to Europe, enrolled in the universities, worked in the laboratories and institutes. The advanced industrial structure of France and Britain supplied the model for Japanese factory builders. The modern Japanese army was a replica of Germany's; the Japanese navy of Britain's, the mightiest in the world.

The frenzy to Westernize seemed to have no limits. Improvement Societies sprang up everywhere, unanimous in their disdain and even contempt for Japan's age-old customs, habits, and ideas. Fanatics advocated intermarriage with the whites in order to "improve the race." More sober reformers praised Western science with its marvelous inventions: lantern slides, photography, the talking machine or phonograph. Journalists rivaled poets in their lush descriptions of gas and kerosene that were replacing candles and whale oil. In 1877 the first telephone line was built between Tokyo and Yokohama. Ten years later electricity like some great torch of man-made lightning illuminated the dark nights of two thousand years.

Among the many Westernizers Fukuzawa Yukichi was probably the most notable. He wrote some hundred books and pamphlets popularizing Western knowledge. When he traveled to the United States he brought back a *Webster's English Dictionary* and founded an English language school. Impressed by the English twenty-six-letter alphabet he attempted to reform the Japanese written language where ideas are communicated by *eighty thousand* ideograms. Why couldn't two or three thousand be enough? he asked.

When Emperor Meiji died in 1912, Japan, like one of her own legendary heroes, had leaped out of feudalism to become a modern state — Tokyo, formerly Yedo, the capital of a world power. The name Tokyo is made up of two ideograms: *To* means "east"; *Kyo* means "capital." Tokyo, the East or Eastern Capital.

Beefsteaks, short hair, Western costumes, factories, phonographs, shipyards, battleships — no Western innovation charmed so many Japanese as the railroad. British engineers had constructed the first Japanese railroad in 1872, connecting Tokyo and Yokohama. The emperor and his court climbed aboard the "steam vehicle" and as the excited crowds gaped, the locomotive puffed black clouds of smoke like a dragon in a Japanese folk tale. Within twenty years, Japanese engineers had laced their mountainous country with steel track, bored tunnels through rock, and spanned the innumerable short rushing rivers with bridges. Today, railroads and travel are as popular as they ever were in the nineteenth century. Americans jump into an automobile, the Japanese settle down in a railroad carriage: old people going to visit some Buddhist temple; youngsters bound for a skiing trip in the mountains; schoolchildren on a tour of their country's historical monuments.

The West! Back in the 1870's it was like a messianic religion few Japanese could resist. There were extremists who actually became arsonists, setting fire to Buddhist temples and ancient palaces. Opposed to these were the diehards who refused to abandon the old Japanese traditions. The story of Taki Zenzaburo, the governor of Kobe, has become a legend. His hatred of the West became uncontrollable and one day he ordered his soldiers to fire on the "barbarians." When Emperor Meiji learned the facts he asked Taki Zenzaburo to commit hari-kari or ritual suicide. Seven European observers, like reporters in an electrocution chamber, witnessed the grisly self-execution. As was the old custom, Taki Zenzaburo disemboweled himself.

While Japan had modernized herself with astonishing speed, her great neighbor China continued to sleep the sleep of four thousand years. Nobody knows how old Chinese civilization is. If we arbitrarily decide to use writing as a measure, we can fix a date as long ago as 1600 B.C. Unlike Japan, China had failed to change

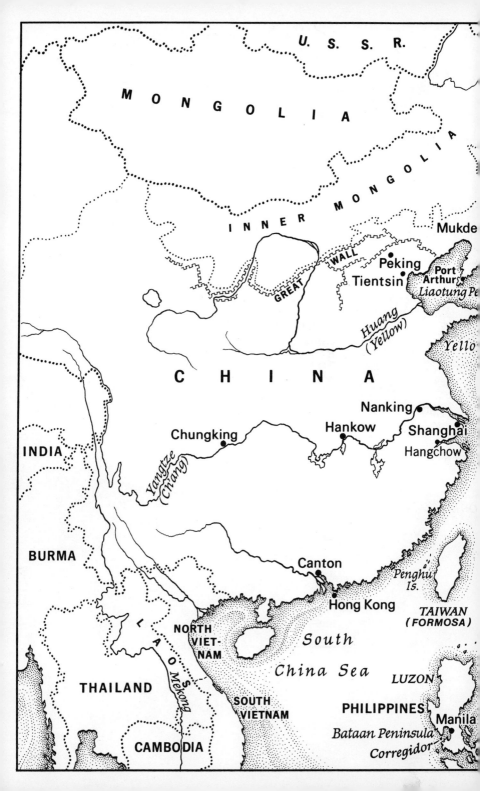

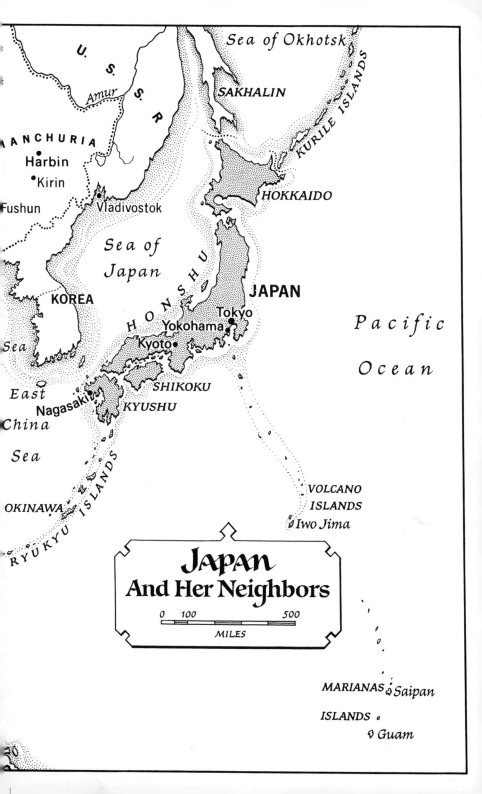

her ancient ways. Like Japan, China had also tried to keep out the strange bearded men who had first ventured to her shores. But still they came. To Britain, France, Tsarist Russia, and the United States in the nineteenth century, China was another backward nation to subjugate, to possess, to colonize.

Japan in the 1870's, like an outsider at a feast, looked on as the Westerners tore vast China apart like a roast duck. In 1874, Japan grabbed a piece: the island of Formosa or present-day Taiwan. Liking the taste, her admirals and generals cast a greedy eye at the Chinese protectorate of Korea.

A hundred miles of water separated the Korean peninsula from the southernmost Japanese island of Kyushu. Japanese cruisers steamed into Korea's waters and attacked the Chinese war junks. The Sino-Japanese War of 1894–1895 could have only one conclusion. For how could the "half-deads," as the Japanese mockingly called the Chinese, resist any modern military power.

The defeated Manchu emperor of China ceded Korea, the Penghu islands, and the Liaotung peninsula to the Japanese. In China, there was rage, frustration, and fear that the nation would be devoured like another Africa. A new patriotic organization, the Society of Righteous and Harmonious Fists — known in the West as the "Boxers" — took to the streets, shouting slogans:

"Save the Manchu dynasty and exterminate the foreign devils!"

The Western nations, including Tsarist Russia and Japan, formed an international army in 1900, invaded China, and captured Peking. They burned the Boxer headquarters, executed any man suspected of membership, and imposed a new and humiliating treaty on China. The protocol of 1901, in effect, forced the Manchu emperor to act as a policeman in the service of the "foreign devils" against his own subjects.

The Russians hadn't been too happy at the emergence of the Japanese. Britain, France, and the United States, however, had welcomed the Japanese as a counterweight to Tsarist influence in the Far East. British and American bankers in London and New York had floated loans to finance Japanese military expansion. In 1902, the Anglo-Japanese Alliance infuriated the Tsar and he decided to smash its Japanese partner.

Russian troops, stationed in Manchuria, marched into northern Korea. In St. Petersburg, the Tsarist capital, the alarmed Japanese envoys attempted to appease the aroused Russian bear. They proposed the division of Manchuria and Korea into two separate "spheres of influence" — a hypocritical diplomatic phrase for colonies. The Russians refused. On February 6, 1904, Tokyo recalled her representatives at the Russian court. Two days later, without a formal declaration of war, the Japanese launched a three-pronged military operation. Admiral Togo's fleet steamed toward Korea. Admiral Uryu, an Annapolis graduate, convoyed Japanese infantrymen to the peninsula. In the north, Japanese torpedo boats attacked Port Arthur, the greatest Russian bastion in the Far East.

On February 10, the Japanese declared war — the Russo-Japanese War of 1904–1905 — denouncing the Russian designs on Korea which they compared to a dagger, "pointed at the heart of Japan."

Port Arthur with its forts and powerful Russian fleet was the main objective of the Japanese strategists. A Russian squadron was lured out of the harbor and demolished. The Russian flagship, racing for safety, hit a Japanese mine and sank, drowning officers and crew. Meanwhile, General Nogi's Third Army advanced on Port Arthur and captured a key hill that commanded a view of the besieged city and harbor. Nogi's artillery began to shell Port Arthur and the bottled-up Russian fleet. The siege was long and bloody before the Japanese gained the greatest prize of the war. On January 5, 1905, the Russian commander surrendered with all his officers and men.

Twenty thousand Japanese soldiers had been killed but now their victorious general was free to join forces with the Japanese armies in Manchuria. Four hundred thousand Japanese clashed with three hundred and fifty thousand Russians along a hundred-mile front. The Battle of Mukden raged for three weeks. Again, the Japanese were the victors. They had suffered seventy-one thousand casualties in killed and wounded but the Russians had paid far more dearly. Eighty-nine thousand of their fighting men had been either killed or wounded.

The Russian bear, bleeding, still hoped to win the final victory. From Kronstadt on the North Sea, the Russian Baltic Fleet had hoisted anchor in October 1904, bound for Vladivostok on the Pacific. Month after month the Baltic Fleet steamed eastward to the coasts of French Indochina, and then through the Korean Straits. On May 27 and 28, the Russian and Japanese fleets clashed in a great sea battle. The double-headed-eagle flags of the Tsar and the Rising Sun flags of the Japanese emperor waved in the wind while down below on the cleared decks the cannon roared. Before it was over, the Russian bear had almost literally been sent to the bottom of the sea; twelve thousand sailors and officers had gone down with their ships. The Russians had lost six battleships, six cruisers, five destroyers, and many other craft.

The magnitude of the Japanese victory at sea astonished the entire world. The United States and Britain, who had secretly sided with the Japanese, now began to ask troubling questions. Had they been right in supporting Tokyo against St. Petersburg?

President Theodore Roosevelt mediated between Russia and Japan at Portsmouth, New Hampshire. The New England town had been chosen because of its cool climate; Washington, D.C., that August, was sweltering. At Portsmouth, the two warring nations signed a peace treaty. Japan was granted "paramount political, military, and economic interests in Korea."

It could be said that Tsarist Russia had also signed its death warrant at Portsmouth. The Russians had not only hoped to crush Japan but sought also to divert the revolutionary discontent of the workers and peasants. A patriotic war against "the race of yellow monkeys," as the Tsarist ministers called the Japanese, had seemed an ideal solution. But instead of victory there was utter defeat. In the Russian cities the workers staged demonstrations and clashed with the Cossacks in armed revolt.

The revolution of 1905 was suppressed but in another dozen years it would flare up again, uncontrollable, to destroy tsar and empire. New men who called themselves Bolsheviks or Communists seized power. The imperial city of Petrograd would be renamed for one of them — Lenin.

1905 was a turning point in world history. For the first time in the Age of Machinery, an Asiatic people had mustered its armor against the all-conquering white man and defeated him — an armor manufactured by Japanese workers in Japanese war plants. Admiral Togo and General Nogi, the nation's heroes, like the shoguns of the past, merely had to nod their heads for an entire people to bow in homage. Huge sums of money were allocated to the military. The samurai sword, modernized for modern warfare, glittered over all Asia.

When Japan in 1910 boldly annexed Korea, the West looked on with more and more misgivings. When and where would Japanese expansion stop? The questions became more and more bitter. The United States, once so sympathetic to Japanese ambitions, turned cold. And the racist phrase — "the Yellow Peril" — began to echo through the land.

# TWO

# The Land of the Rising Sun

TSARIST RUSSIA, larger than the entire continent of South America, was a Goliath among the nations of the world. And yet, like the Biblical Goliath, it had been struck down by a David arisen from the Japanese islands.

Public opinion in the West shifted against the Japanese. Statesmen, journalists, and ordinary citizens felt and voiced a new hostility. The racists coined ugly epithets. But epithets have always concealed rather than revealed the national characteristics of a people.

Intelligent men in Moscow, London, Paris, and Washington dismissed the anti-Japanese slurs to ask penetrating questions. What forces in Japanese history had molded the Japanese character? What made them so unique? What differentiated them from the Chinese, and Indians, and the other Orientals, none of whom had been able to defend themselves against the white man? Unlike huge China or India, Japan was a small country. The Japanese possessed no rich colonial empire like the British or the French. They had built their formidable war machine on a mountainous archipelago in the northern Pacific whose four largest islands could have fitted into a corner of either the Chinese or Russian empires.

Honshu, the largest island — 88,930 square miles — was about the size of the state of Minnesota. Hokkaido — 30,077 square miles — was about the size of Maine. Kyushu with its 16,215 square miles and Shikoku with its 7,240 square miles were the equivalent of three New Jerseys. All four of these major islands were somewhat smaller than the state of California.

All were mountainous with few mineral resources except coal. They lacked grasslands to raise herds; the tillable soil was no more than 20 percent of the total land area. In the heavy population centers, the climate was similar to the climate prevalent in the American belt of cities stretching from Boston to Baltimore: cold winters and hot summers. The regular rains were definitely a "natural resource" for they insured plentiful rice crops. Nature, otherwise, was fickle; earthquakes were a constant threat. No man could tell when the earth might cleave open. For centuries the wooden buildings had been built with interlocking beams like ships designed to ride out rough seas. In 1923, Tokyo was demolished and more than sixty thousand of its residents killed.

Sixty miles from the capital, snowcapped Mount Fujiyama — 12,388 feet above sea level — had inspired generations of artists and poets. Yet destructive fire lurked in its volcanic depths. The goddess of fire, the Japanese believed, had her dwelling place in their sacred mountain. Fujiyama, dormant since 1707, symbolized both the beauty and the menace that had always been a part of the Japanese landscape.

Threatened by earthquake, fire, flood, and tidal wave, dependent on limited rice fields for their bread, the rough seas for their fish, these island people were nevertheless destined to shake the world. There had been signs and omens. Six years before the war with Tsarist Russia, the "dwarf-men," as the Chinese dubbed the Japanese, had defeated still another Goliath: imperial China.

The Japanese islands, on the map, look like a five-legged dragon whose head is the northernmost island of Hokkaido; the neck and body Honshu; the five legs formed by the two southerly islands of Kyushu and Shikoku, and the three peninsulas jutting out of Honshu. There are almost a thousand smaller islands, some no bigger than wave-drenched rocks. The Sea of Japan separates the Japanese islands from Soviet Asia, Man-

churia, and Korea. Southward, below the island of Kyushu and the Ryuku island chain, the East China Sea lies like a great waterway between China and the Japanese ports.

A sea dragon — Japan — stretched from the subarctic to the subtropical, and its appetite would become insatiable in the Second World War. Defeated finally, all her war-conquered territories taken away, reduced to the size she had been in 1868 — people everywhere agreed that Japan was "through." Yet, within twenty years, this shrunken and devastated nation would rise out of the ashes to become the world's third strongest economic power, surpassed only by the United States and the Soviet Union.

Who in 1945 could imagine such a phenomenal recovery?

Once more the old questions were asked: "How did they do it . . . what is there in the Japanese? . . ."

To answer these questions we must go back in time.

The Japanese ability to work, to learn, to make war, had their beginnings in an age before written history.

"The islands were first inhabited in comparatively recent times — perhaps five thousand years ago." This was the conclusion of Sir George Sansom, one of the greatest Western authorities on Japan. Few scholars, whether Westerners or Japanese, would disagree. The archaeological evidence speaks for itself. No old Stone

Age tools or weapons have ever been unearthed in Japan. Those that have been dug up were fashioned, so to speak, only yesterday — in the late Stone Age when men had learned how to finish and polish stone. The Ainus were the original inhabitants, migrants from northern Asia where they had hunted and fished along the shores of the Sea of Okhotsk, or "The Sea Left Behind" in the Ainu language. Racially, the Ainus were a Caucasian type, white aborigines, bearded and hairy. They would never attain the civilization of the yellowish-skinned Asiatics who migrated at some later period from Korea and southern China. Like the American Indians they followed the ways of their ancestors. They believed that the bears they killed for meat were actually human beings. To appease the spirits of the slain beast-humans they performed special rites. Primitive-souled men, they were no match for the seafaring Asiatics who came ashore in the southern islands. The newcomers were hunters and fishers, too. But unlike the Ainus they learned how to farm the land. And from the rice they grew, a magical seed sprouted, the seed that would produce cities and civilization.

To the rice-growing tribes, the Ainus were *ebisu* or barbarians to be driven into the wild mountains.

The best soil was concentrated on the island of Honshu. It lay in three great plains, the largest of which was the plain of Kanto with an area of five thousand square miles. The plain of Ise covered six hundred square miles; that of Kinto five hundred square miles. Throughout early Japanese history, the leaders of the rice-growing clans fought for their possession. And as the centuries passed, the clan leaders wore silken robes and lived in castles, no longer semi-barbarian chieftains but nobles. Finally, the most powerful of the nobles assumed the prerogatives of an emperor.

Rice was both wealth and civilization. Rice fed the peasants and the craftsmen, the samurai and the nobles. The peasants also grew barley and millet but the favorite grain was rice. They planted mulberry trees whose leaves provided food for silkworms. The craftsmen wove silk and miners brought gold out of the mountains — never too much of it, but sufficient for the rings and ornaments cherished by the nobles and their ladies. Sufficient, too, to gild the chambers of the Imperial Household.

Rice was the true gold and inevitably the first imperial court was on the plain of Ise at Nara (A.D. 710–784); the second on the plain of Kinto at Kyoto (794–1868); the third at Tokyo in 1868, with the Meiji restoration, on the great plain of Kanto.

The dense forests of evergreen, cypress, camphor, and bamboo supplied the basic building materials for palace and mansion, temple and shrine, house and hut. The offshore waters, warmed by the "Black Current," teemed with fish, lobsters, and oysters. The mountainous islands themselves, according to an old myth, rested on the backs of gigantic fish deep in the sea.

Myth and history, fact and legend, were all woven together in the first Japanese books — the *Kojiki* or "Record of Ancient Matters" written in A.D. 712 and the *Nihon-shoki* or "Chronicles of Japan" written in A.D. 720. These two works are the chief source of everything we know about early Japan. They can be compared to a fabulous tapestry whose figures include supernatural heroes and dragons, as well as real-life emperors and poets.

The *Kojiki* and the *Nihon-shoki,* like the Old Testament, told the story of the creation of the universe. Yet, how profoundly different from our Bible! No divine creator appears to shape heaven and earth out of chaos; there is no Garden of Eden; no Adam and Eve. In the beginning, according to the Japanese chroniclers, there was the Plain of Heaven on which dwelled the gods, nameless and misty figures. Then a celestial pair appeared, the god Izanagi and his sister, the goddess Izanami. If Izanami seems Eve-like, the life-force in her staggers the imagination, for like Mother Nature she gave birth not only to gods, but to islands, mountains, rivers, to all natural phenomena. Then, like a mortal woman, the goddess Izanami died. Her celestial brother tried to find her. His quest took him to the Land of

Darkness where he found the rotting remains of his sister. Returning to earth, he purified himself by bathing in a stream.

Today, no Westerner in Japan fails to be astonished by the cleanliness of the Japanese. The Japanese, in turn, regard our habits of personal hygiene as barbarous. First, they scrub themselves clean of dirt *before* stepping into a tub. Their bathrooms, unlike ours, do not have toilets, which are in another room. The Japanese bathroom is a place for relaxation and meditation. As in ancient times, the tub is often made of unpainted wood, the most beautiful of materials to the Japanese. There were also stone baths in the inns, as well as outdoor baths in tranquil surroundings where the bather could look at trees and flowers, a brook, a lake, a gorge. All these very Japanese customs go back to the springtime of the gods who purified themselves by bathing in mountain streams. They still exist in modern Japan: a continuity with the remote past that we in the West have lost.

Of all the gods who issued out of Izanami, the most wondrous was the sun goddess, Amaterasu. Her shrine at Ise is the greatest in Japan. The Japanese, like the ancient Egyptians and Incas, worshiped the sun as the source of life and believed that their supreme rulers traced their lineage back to the golden sphere that rose in the east at dawn. If we admire sunset, they admire sunrise. The flag of Japan — the Land of the Rising Sun — is both a national and a religious symbol; the Japanese emperor a semireligious figure, the Tenno or King of Heaven, a priestly intermediary between his people and the ultimate mysteries of creation. To the Japanese pilot or soldier in the Second World War death was no enemy if one died for the emperor. Their fierce military spirit had its origins in age-old beliefs.

The first Emperor Jimmu, we are told in the *Kojiki*, ascended the throne in 660 B.C. Modern scholars place this event some four centuries later but there is general agreement that by the year A.D. 400 Japan had become a unified nation in which the emperor occupied the central position. All institutions, all classes — nobles, samurai, peasants — revolved about the Tenno like planets about the sun.

The Imperial Court lived on the island of Honshu in today's province of Yamato. And when modern historians refer to the Japan that still lacked a written language they use the phrase, "Yamato times." Writing would come from China as well as the Buddhist religion and the philosophy of Confucius.

The Yamato rulers — 200 B.C. to A.D. 300 — governed a nation whose religion, Shinto, was a form of nature worship. We might have expected the Shinto deities to be fierce and even bloodthirsty — not gentle and mild as they were — in a land where nature was hard. A land of earthquakes and typhoons and fires where the monsoons blew year after year, inundating the coastal villages, and where the wooden cities burned, set ablaze by natural causes or by the torches of warring men.

The Aztecs of Mexico tore out the hearts of men, women, and children to appease their gods. The Hebrews feared Jehovah; the early Christians symbolically ate the flesh and drank the blood of Jesus Christ in wafer and wine.

The gods of Shinto seem to make few demands on their worshipers. Although superior to men, they can sicken or die like ordinary mortals, and commit all sorts of mistakes; they are happy-go-lucky deities who even take vacations. In modern Japan, October is "the month without gods" when all of them, like some big family, journey to Izumo for a reunion.

True, as gods and goddesses, they possessed *kami* or power but they didn't monopolize it. There was *kami* in the sun, in mountains, in tigers, in extraordinary human beings, heroes and sages. *Kami* was a universal force. If the first Emperor Jimmu possessed *kami* so did the humble dead. We in the West call this ancestor worship but this is only half the truth.

To the Japanese, life and death, the forces of nature, the genius of man, are all passengers in a mysterious common boat that can sail the sea, or the wind, or even the breath of a child. We divide everything into neat little boxes: past and present, good and evil, paradise and hell, God in his heaven and man on earth. The Japanese, like most Asiatics, see the world as open-ended, without partitions.

Primitive Shinto rites took place outdoors where the gods were offered grain and fruit. No animals were sacrificed because blood was regarded as polluting, as were wounds, disease, uncleanliness, and death. After mourning the death of a loved one, the entire family cleansed themselves in a purifying bath. When Buddhism, a far more complex religion, came to Japan, Shinto still maintained its hold on the Japanese mind and heart.

Today, there are more than a hundred thousand Shinto shrines in Japan. Like the church towers of Europe they are everywhere. Most of them are made of unpainted wood or natural stone. The shrine where the spirit of the god dwells is usually a simple building of cypress wood with a slanted, thatched roof. It is approached through three gateways or *torii;* sometimes through two or even one. No religious structure could be simpler than these "god-gates." Two upright posts with a single or double crossbar — they seem like perches for birds.

Shinto, like some mystical mirror, reflected nature, the unity of bird and tree, mountain and forest. The most typical rite — the *matsuri* — may celebrate a good harvest, honoring Inari, the god of rice (sometimes Inari changes sex to become the goddess of rice.) Or the *matsuri* will honor a man's ancestors who had once loved and passed on the priceless gift of human existence. The *matsuri* will end with songs and dances, or what we would call "fun and games." Other rites and festivals pay homage to the trades and professions, or commemorate historical events. Every city and town has its own special celebrations, bright with flower processions and led by Shinto priests in plain red, yellow, or white robes. Every aspect of Shinto links the gods to the world, to men working in rice field or factory, and finally to the mystery of life itself.

Today, some twenty-eight million Japanese out of a population of one hundred and five million live and work in the huge factory cities of Tokyo, Yokohama, Osaka, and Kobe, where the smokestacks have turned the sky into a brownish-gray pall: a skywriting whose message is unmistakable.

"We have Westernized ourselves," thoughtful Japanese say. "The question is will we be able to absorb what we have learned as we once absorbed what we learned from ancient China? Or will we become industrial robots not too different from industrial robots everywhere?"

The color prints of centuries ago have preserved another Japan of natural and unspoiled beauty. Woods and lakes, mountains and rivers, monasteries and *torii,* the "god-gates" of a people who once lived in harmony with nature, a people whose ancestors had mastered the arts and sciences of China and remained Japanese.

# THREE

# The Chinese Flowering

CENTURIES BEFORE the birth of Christ, the first Chinese travelers journeyed eastward to the court of the King of Heaven. The people they met thought of themselves not as Japanese, but as men of Yamato. There in the central provinces of Honshu island, the imperial throne had established itself. There myth had become history.

Like a cherry tree, the Yamato civilization was rooted in the soil of Honshu. It would be transformed when the great flower of China was grafted to it. But always the new blossoms would retain the Yamato shape and fragrance.

The very name Japan or Nippon, as the Japanese call their country, is derived from the Chinese *Jih-pen,* which means, "source of the sun."

The Chinese came from a land they proudly called the Central Realm; they believed their vast empire to be the true center of the world, geographically and spiritually. Chinese arts and sciences, philosophy and statecraft, had penetrated to all the kingdoms bordering on the Central Realm. Among them was Korea, the long peninsula jutting out of Manchuria.

Washed by the Yellow Sea on the west, the Sea of Japan on the east, Korea was the "bridge" to Kyushu, the westernmost of the Japanese islands. Long before the first Chinese visitors, Korean traders had crossed the hundred miles of sea between their country and Kyushu, a three- or four-day trip if the weather was favorable, weeks if the weather was rough. They introduced bronze weapons and tools to Kyushu and, later on, iron weapons. These metal axes and spears gave the edge to the tribal chieftains and warriors of Kyushu over the Ainus with their bone and stone weapons.

Metalworking, too, had originated in the Central Realm, the treasure-house of knowledge for all Asia. Generations of Chinese scholars, the mandarins, had recorded the thousand and one achievements of an advanced society whose people had been literate as far back as the Shang dynasty ( 1600–1122 B.C. ). There were libraries in the Chinese cities, the books made out of bamboo and silk, which were expensive materials.

Then in A.D. 105, a Chinese official invented the world's first paper, a composite of flax, bark, and old fishing nets. Chinese papermaking would spread to India, and eventually to all the lands encircling the Central Realm. The earliest surviving accounts of Yamato times were written by Chinese scribes in A.D. 100. To them, the illiterate men of Yamato seemed like barbarians. Nevertheless they couldn't help being impressed by the strong central government, the strict discipline, the cleanliness of noble and peasant, the rites and ceremonies of Shinto.

The Korean "bridge" became a two-way road. Yamato officials sailed from Kyushu to Korea and continued their travels into China. They marveled at the sights and sounds they saw: irrigation systems and huge earthen dikes in the country, palaces and temples in the cities, and among all the wonders, the magic of Chinese writing that enabled men "to speak without tongues."

The Chinese written language, unlike our own, is not alphabetic. Every idea, every object is represented by an ideogram. Long, long ago, Chinese ideograms were simplified drawings or pictures. A mountain would be represented by its peak; a house by its roof. There were tens of thousands of different ideograms. Today, a knowledge of three thousand is necessary in order to read a Japanese newspaper. A child in Tokyo will spend the first six years at school learning how to write and read a thousand ideograms. He will write with a brush, not a pen, and that is why calligraphy has been called an art. Innumerable ideograms could be miniature, abstract paintings.

Spoken Japanese, contrary to Western belief, is utterly unlike spoken Chinese. It is as different as Finnish is different from English, French, or German. Written Japanese, however, is a combination of Yamato and Chinese. When the Yamato scholars adopted the Chinese written language, they also learned and began to use thousands of Chinese words. By the year A.D. 400 the islanders, at last, could also speak "without tongues."

There was no end to the Chinese imports. In A.D. 552, the first Buddhist monks arrived, preaching a new religion. They brought the Buddhist scriptures and Buddhist art works. Other travelers introduced the teachings of the great Chinese sage Confucius.

"The Great Change," as it would be called by the Japanese, forever altered the practices, customs, and habits of a thousand years. Nothing would be the same afterwards; neither government, religion, art, nor architecture.

Chinese Buddhism had originated in India. Five hundred years before the birth of Christ, a wise man by the name of Sakyamuni — the Buddha — had meditated on life and concluded that only the mind existed.

All else was illusion. Man and insect, bird and flower, forest and mountain, all living things and all inanimate things were transient shapes, infinite variations of the absolute or Nirvana. "Just as in the vast ethereal sphere, stars and darkness, light and mirage . . . become visible, and vanish again like the features of a dream — so everything endowed with an individual shape is to be regarded."

Buddhism, unlike the Christian, Hebrew, or Islamic faiths, was a religion without miracles. From India it had spread to China and all Asia. In Japan, Buddhism would be all-pervasive for eight centuries — from A.D. 700 to A.D. 1500 — absorbing, or more accurately, merging with Shinto: a mixture of rites and prayers, thoughts and books. The Buddhist doctrine of continuous change and rebirth appealed to a people who had always felt the unity of man and nature, the living and the dead. Shinto-Buddhism, as the Japanese themselves said, was really a single religion, "with two faces."

Buddhism, at first, won its converts at the Yamato court. The peasants and artisans remained faithful to Shinto, and to the Shinto gods. If the Buddhist scriptures were closed books to the illiterate folk, the new architecture and art evoked their admiration. Few man-built structures can equal the elegance of the many-storied pagoda; each tapering story decreasing in size toward the top. The Chinese pagoda was built of stone, the Japanese of wood, but both enchant the eye and mind.

Many writers, Westerners and Orientals, have described the heaven-soaring beauty of the pagoda in which the Buddha was honored and his preachings observed. To the Italian scholar Fosco Maraini, the pagoda seemed like a huge butterfly, "settled in the middle of a wood, ready at any moment to resume its capricious flight."

Buddhist architecture and art cast a spell over a people who had been master craftsmen for centuries: silk makers and embroiderers, fan makers and woodcarvers, gold- and silversmiths. The influence on the native sculptors and artists was profound. We can imagine their delight when they looked at the innumerable statues of Buddha and the Buddhist gods in bronze, wood, or delicate porcelain. How awed they must have been as they stood before the serenity and majesty of the Buddha. What emotions they must have felt as they studied the host of lesser deities, representing all the forces, good and evil, that enveloped man and his world. Kwannon, the god of mercy, was sometimes depicted with eleven heads, ten of them joined together like a crown resting on top of the eleventh. Bishamon, one of the seven gods of luck, was portrayed with a pagoda in one hand, the symbol of religious faith, and a spear symbolizing warrior zeal in the other. Hotei, another god of luck, who might have been a Santa Claus to our eyes, was a jolly god whose immense belly indicated his good nature.

The Japanese sculptors and artists, however, weren't mere imitators. Their view of earthly existence had been formed by the realities of their rugged, mountainous islands, the recurrent disasters of earthquake and flood, the centuries of warfare against the Ainus, the conflicts between the noble clans, the courage and honor of a few as opposed to the greed and treachery of the many. If their works idealized the Buddhist deities, they nevertheless portrayed them as men and women.

Like all human institutions, Buddhism had its contradictions. If some orders despised the false glory of the world, building their monasteries in the mountains, still others, like the knights of Christian Europe, brawled and intrigued for power; their city monasteries were armed camps. "Buddha preached eighty-four thousand doctrines," the realistic Japanese declared, not in rebellion but with calm acceptance. Shingon, a variant of Buddhism, erected ornate temples crowded with bronze gods and furies. Tendai Buddhism maintained that Buddha could be found in a dewdrop. And in centuries to come, Zen Buddhism — "blood Buddhism," as Western students would observe — denounced books and bookish knowledge, a philosophy that appealed to the sword-wielding samurai.

The first Buddhist commandment is: "Thou shalt not take life." Every year, ceremonies celebrating the sacredness of life were held in which caged birds and animals were released. And yet, as in every society, somebody had to do the dirty work. In Japan, the *eta* performed the tasks considered to be the lowest and most degrading in a Buddhist culture. Butchers, tanners, street cleaners — despised and hated like the untouchables of present-day India.

The new religion had transformed Japan. But, as always, Buddhist monastery and Shinto shrine, palace and hut, rested on pillars of rice. Not even the most fanatical Buddhist disputed the worship accorded to the Shinto god of rice, Inari. The Japanese word *gohan* or "boiled rice" is also the word for "a meal." A meal without rice was unthinkable to both peasant and noble. Taxes were paid in rice; rice continued to be a sort of gold.

The historical Buddha had lived at about the same time as Confucius. The great sage during his lifetime, 551–479 B.C., had attracted students from every section of China. He instructed them in music, rites, archery, chariot-driving, mathematics, and writing. His ideal was to create "men of perfect virtue" who would take their place in an ideal society. Confucius was a humanist, not what we would call a democrat. He advocated a strong state where sons obeyed their fathers, peasants their masters, and where all Chinese bowed to the emperor. Late in his life, he began compiling the ancient Chinese books that would become known as the "Classics." Edited by Confucius, they became the texts every educated Chinese had to study. Candidates for governmental positions had to pass examinations based on the "Classics." These men, the mandarins, were equivalent to a civil service.

Confucius would be worshiped as a god by future generations in China. In 1934 the Kuomintang party of Chiang Kai-shek revived Confucianism as a religion to counteract Chinese Communist ideology.

According to Confucius, men had duties, not rights. This basic principle dominated the thinking of the Tang dynasty, A.D. 618–906, and the Tang emperors of China. In A.D. 645, the Japanese Emperor Kotoku decided to model his regime after the Chinese Tang. He initiated the many changes that would be known as the Taikwa Reform. An imperial army supplanted the age-old feudal musters of soldiers; provincial governors replaced the feudal lords. Discriminatory laws that favored the highborn against the lowborn were abolished in favor of a more just system. A new bureaucracy was created, in which rank was indicated by different hats and buttons.

The Tang capital of Ch'ang-an was regarded as the jewel of the world. Kotoku's architects drew up the plans for a second Ch'ang-an. Like Ch'ang-an, the Japanese capital of Nara, A.D. 710–784, was a checkerboard of avenues and streets crisscrossing at right angles. Surrounded by hills and streams, its natural beauty enhanced by an architecture imperial in its palaces, religious in its temples — Nara would inspire generations of poets. Walls encircled the palaces and each imposing monastery consisted of seven related buildings: pagoda, library, belfry, lecture hall, oratory, dining hall, and a dormitory for the Buddhist monks.

Nara, like the Rome of the Popes, was the holy city of Buddhism. The many religious establishments soon attained a secular power that threatened the imperial throne. Both the Buddhist monks and the nobles resented the Taikwa Reform. Their intrigues and plots grew more and more audacious. Following a smallpox epidemic in A.D. 737, the emperor was persuaded to build a colossal statue of the Buddha Roshana or "He who enlightens." Five hundred tons of brass, eight tons of lead and zinc, went into this fifty-foot-high effigy. Each piece was cast on the spot and gilded with gold newly discovered in Ainu country. Supposedly, the Buddha Roshana would intercede against future plagues. During the ceremonies of its installation in the Hall of the Great Image, the Buddhist priests succeeded in establishing Buddhism as the state religion: "Of all the various laws, the Great Word of the Buddha is the most excellent for protecting the state."

Huge sculptures such as the Buddha Roshana are exceptional in Japan. Whether working in bronze, brass, gold, wood, or ivory, Japanese artists have always had an affinity for the small. The miniature *netsuke* is far more typical; the first netsuke were toggles or devices used to secure or hold carved buttons or bottle stoppers, humble beginnings for an art form that finally achieved masterpieces. A typical netsuke might depict all seven gods of luck, sailing on a treasure ship, and still be small enough to fit into a child's palm.

The nobles collected netsuke and patronized all the arts. Some fancied themselves as poets, and like so many other Japanese throughout the centuries, they described clouds and moonlight, snow and rain, bamboo grove and cherry blossom: nature was their theme. When they returned from expeditions against the bearded Ainu who had never ceased harassing the frontier garrisons, their poems recalled the brevity of life, the fury of war, the duties of a warrior. "On the hills our corpses shall rot in the grass . . ." This is one line of a famous poem written in the middle of the eighth century.

In Nara, the Buddhists steadily accumulated wealth and land. Crafty monks concocted new schemes as they sipped tea which they believed stimulated and sharpened the intellect and all the senses.

The tea, too, had come from China. Inescapable, the Chinese presence towered even higher than the Buddha Roshana. The peasants, laboring in the rice fields, feared both their robed masters and the supernatural *oni* or horned Chinese devils. The *oni* could be red or blue or gray or some other color but their character never varied; they were always cruel and lustful creatures, unlike the *tengu* who reflected the kindliness of the Shinto gods. Half-bird, half-human, the *tengu* wore round black hats and excelled as swordsmen. They lived in trees high in the mountains, mischievous beings but never evil. The peasants, oppressed by monk and noble, told tales of gallant *tengu* who in olden times had aided the weak and the sick. Still other tales told of the clever fox who could if he wished change into a human, a gift he shared with the badger and the serpent.

Nara remained the capital for almost a century. But finally the power of the militant Buddhist orders became intolerable to the Emperor Kammu. He decided to build a new city some twenty-five miles to the north of Nara. It was called Heian or "Peace and Tranquility."

Today, Kyoto, the City of Purple Hills, occupies the same site as ancient Heian. (To avoid confusion I will use the later name of Kyoto, the capital of Japan for almost a thousand years, from 794 to 1868.)

Like Nara or the Chinese Ch'ang-an, Kammu's new capital had wide avenues and narrower intersecting streets; another checkerboard in design. The palace, the government halls, the pavilions and gardens, were enclosed behind walls like a city within a city. Buddhist temples were constructed and consecrated.

Although Nara was close, a long day's ride by horse, it seemed very distant to the emperor and his court. For years, building activities continued; a new university was established with departments in mathematics, law, and Chinese letters. Confucian studies would dominate the curriculum as at all Japanese universities. But the cool logic of the Confucian "Classics" would always be counterbalanced by Buddhist mysticism. The Japanese mind and heart couldn't help responding to such Buddhist precepts as *essence* and *reincarnation,* so similar to the old Shinto ideas of *kami* or power, and the oneness of man and nature.

Emperor Kammu was a strong ruler. When he walked into his state room — an immense chamber, two hundred feet long and fifty wide — he cast a truly imperial shadow. No highborn noble or Buddhist dignitary dared to oppose him; not openly anyway. During his reign (781–806) imperial prestige reached a zenith. Nevertheless, the Taikwa Reform, like so many other reforms throughout history, West or East, had already begun to disintegrate. It died during the reigns of Kammu's successors.

# FOUR

# The Samurai and the Poets

*F*ROM EARLIEST TIMES there were two Japans: the Japan of the warrior and the Japan of the poet. Together, they wrote the history of their nation; the warrior or samurai with sword in hand, the poet with brush and black ink.

Long before there was a written language, tribal warriors armed with bone-tipped lances had battled the Ainu. Their descendants, wearing iron battle masks painted with red lacquer like the faces of demons, had fought each other on the rice plains, in the mountains, and on the seas. The sword would dictate the laws of the land for a thousand years. The emperor inherited the three sacred symbols of authority: the mirror, the jewel, the sword. But the *sword* that really mattered was the one wielded by the shoguns or military governors.

And yet shogun and samurai honored the all-wise

Buddha who abhorred blood. They worshiped the kindly Shinto deities in poetic rites where mountain and river, tree and flower, like silent communicants gathered together with mortal men to celebrate the unity of life.

The Japanese, like many other people throughout the world, were divided men, their religious practices separate from the brutal realities of power and power-seeking.

The Taikwa Reform of A.D. 645 had attempted to unify the country under a system of just laws. But after Emperor Kammu's death, the nation, like a ship seized by willful men, sailed where it wished it to go; the emperors, although still revered as semidivine figures, were reduced to glittering figureheads.

By the year 833 one aristocratic family, the Fujiwara, had won control of the state. And as intercourse with China ended, isolating the Japanese islands like so many isolated fortresses in the sea, the Fujiwara influence became supreme. Masters of intrigue, cunning matchmakers whose daughters wedded the emperors, the Fujiwara dictated laws that benefited themselves and the other powerful lords. All these notables mustered private armies to protect their lands and privileges.

It was a feudal world like the Europe of the Middle Ages in which the emperors like the Popes of Rome exercised spiritual if not earthly power. At the imperial court, learned scholars wrote in Chinese just as the medieval scholars of Europe used the Latin of Holy Rome. The poets and romancers, however, employed the native Yamato.

The six books of the *Tale of Genji,* written in the eleventh century by a lady of the court, Murasaki Shikibu, would become the greatest Japanese classic. She narrated the lives and loves of the great nobles and ladies. The hero, the handsome prince Genji, was as irresistible to women as any Hollywood star, but his appreciation of nature was typically Japanese. Poor, suffering Genji! Even when he was depressed, the beauty of a common flower could make him feel that life, after all, was worth living.

Japanese artists, using the simplest means, black ink brushed on white paper, evoked the mystery of cloud and mountain, waterfall and bird. And as in Renaissance Italy where Raphael and Botticelli would seek out living models for their madonnas and saints, Japanese religious painters used very human lords and ladies to render their celestial beings.

"The dwellers above the clouds," as Murasaki Shikibu described her characters, enjoyed every luxury. A host of artisans fabricated their jewel boxes, colored fans, and silken kimonos. Oracles, diviners, and stargazers predicted glorious futures for the perfumed ladies and their lovers. But like all dream worlds, even the Fujiwara centuries (833–1192) couldn't endure forever. Sooner or later, the silken dictatorship had to give way to the naked edge of the sword.

Two great military families, the Taira and the Minamoto, had their own ambitious dreams. As the Fujiwara declined, their rivalry intensified and finally erupted in a civil war that lasted thirty years from 1156 to 1185. At first, the scarlet flag of the Taira triumphed over the white flag of the Minamoto. But as one bloody battle followed another, one of the Minamoto leaders, Yoritomo (1147–1199) emerged as the man of destiny, the inheritor of the future.

Yoritomo was a hard, ruthless soldier, a horseman and swordsman. He had always distrusted the elegant courtiers who waited on the emperor at Kyoto. Now, as the military master of all Japan — the first shogun — he established his permanent headquarters at Kamakura, and called it the *bakufu,* or "camp administration." He died in 1199 at the age of fifty-two, a legend even during his lifetime.

Artists and writers, still unborn, would be fascinated by the leaders of the Minamoto and Taira. Yoritomo, pitiless and courageous, treacherous and magnanimous, had always resented the brilliance of his younger brother Yoshitsune, the pupil, according to the folktales, of the supernatural *tengu.* These birdlike humans had taught him his military skills. Yoshitsune, not Yoritomo, had won the last great battle of the civil war, the sea battle of Dannoura in which the Taira cause had gone down to a watery grave. The Taira defeat, to poets of future times, was preordained by the gods. Taira is also the name of a small crab. Who could doubt that the spirits of the drowned Taira warriors had spiraled down to the bottom of the sea to enter the shell-encased bodies of the *taira* scavenging in the mud?

Perhaps, Yoshitsune, too, had been born under an evil star. His brother, with the war won, plotted ceaselessly to get rid of the hero of Dannoura. The end came in 1189. Surrounded by enemies, his capture inevitable, Yoshitsune killed his wife and children and then committed suicide. The samurai of Yoritomo chopped off Yoshitsune's head, put it inside a black lacquer bowl, and brought the gory trophy to their master.

The fraternal feud would be immortalized in stories and plays, the younger brother portrayed always as the beloved hero hunted like a beast by the older. Artists depicted the tragedy that had divided the two Minamoto leaders — and the still larger tragedy that had divided a nation. They portrayed the famous battles fought by the Minamoto and Taira partisans, the armored samurai on their horses, the *zusa* or foot soldiers with their spears.

No *zusa,* not even the bravest, could hope to become a samurai unless the shogun himself granted permission. Beginning with Yoritomo, the feudal caste system allotted each man his fixed place in a militarized society. The only way the humbly born could rise in the world was to enter one of the Buddhist orders. There as a monk he would receive an education, and if capable or clever, advance in the priesthood.

The *bakufu* at Kamakura recognized one law, one truth, one fact: the sword. The classic *Mirror of the East,* written in the thirteenth century, praised death, if necessary, as preferable to surrender. Less than a century after Yoritomo's death, his successors would be confronted with the greatest threat in the early history of the Land of the Rising Sun.

Kublai Khan, the Mongol emperor of China, conquered the Koreans and looked across the waves at a land he couldn't see: a small kingdom in his opinion, another easy conquest. How could they resist the mighty Khan? His mounted horsemen had brought the scourge of war to three-fourths of Asia. In his arrogance and pride, the dreaded Khan sent his envoys to Japan, demanding submission. They were rebuffed and the Japanese prepared for a life-and-death struggle.

Kublai Khan's first invasion was thwarted. His Mongol warriors had no knowledge of the sea and his Korean vassals no enthusiasm for their master. The Khan sent a mission to Japan, ordering the emperor to come to Peiping, the Chinese capital, and explain the resistance. The Japanese beheaded the Khan's envoys. Immediately the Khan commanded the building of a second invasion fleet. By the year 1280, the Koreans had made a thousand ships; the Chinese some thirty-five hundred junks. Most of them were small but Marco Polo would recall afterwards that a number of them could carry as many as three hundred men with their supplies, weapons, and horses. It is estimated that the combined Korean and Chinese navies had some hundred and fifty thousand warriors on their decks when anchors were hoisted in June 1281.

The time had been carefully chosen. From November to March, the monsoon winds blew down the China coast making the waters too dangerous for sea travel.

Far away, a nation in arms awaited the invaders. And when the sails of the enormous fleet were sighted from the hills of Kyushu, the defenders blinked at what must have seemed like all the ships in the world. "They looked ahead and swallowed their spit," as an old Japanese saying goes. In the temples the bells began to ring — they would ring week after week, all day and all night, as the old people prayed for victory in the fighting that never seemed to end.

The Japanese boats had tried to board the Khan's ships and were cut down. The invaders landed on the beaches and assaulted the Japanese fortifications with catapults and fire attacks. Outnumbered two to one, a hundred and fifty thousand Mongols, Chinese, and Koreans pitted against three hundred thousand samurai and peasant soldiers, the battle raged through the month of July into August. Could the invaders have won? The accounts differ, but all agree that in the second week of August a typhoon roared down on the anchored fleet in the harbor, crashing masts and snapping cables. The Khan's warriors wavered as the sky blackened; the Japanese rushed forward, wielding their swords.

Most of the ships were battered to pieces on the rocks; five hundred survived out of the forty-five hundred that had sailed from Korea. A hundred and thirty thousand warriors and sailors drowned in the mountainous waves or else were hacked and slaughtered on the beaches. Japan had been saved by the *kamikaze,* or "divine wind," as her grateful people called it. They would use the phrase again some six hundred and sixty-four years later to describe the suicidal air pilots — the *kamikaze* — who in order to defeat the enemy crashed their bomb-loaded planes down on the decks of American battleships.

Kublai Khan planned a third invasion but it was never launched. The centuries passed; shogun succeeded shogun. In 1590 Yedo (renamed Tokyo in 1868) became the seat of power for the shogunate. The imperial court remained in Kyoto. The *bakufu* maintained its separate military identity for seven hundred years, from 1185 to 1868, like a Japanese Pentagon. The samurai sword was as much a symbol of Japan as the imperial chrysanthemum or the cherry blossom, the national flower.

"The cherry is the king of flowers, the samurai the king of men."

This old saying speaks for itself and explains the fanatic fighting qualities of the Japanese military in the Second World War. Their discipline and courage had their roots in the *bakufu* state of Yoritomo, the first shogun.

Five hundred years ago, the boy who would become a samurai attended schools we would describe as "tough military preps." He mastered archery, fencing, wrestling, history, literature, and the art of writing. He was trained to obey his superiors in any and all situations, to bow to the lord as the lord bowed to the supreme commander or shogun, the defender of emperor and empire. The future samurai underwent a harsh discipline: to show no emotions; to speak the truth always, for a lie could be punished by death. At fifteen he received the long sword of his profession.

Courage, needless to say, was the supreme virtue: to take one's own life if need be in the rite of *seppuku* or hari-kari by ritual disemboweling. This ritual would be the theme of poems, books, plays, and movies. Just as

we will go to see a Shakespeare play like *Hamlet* or
*Romeo and Juliet,* Japanese will flock to see a 1748
drama based on the old feudal tale of the forty-seven
samurai who committed mass hari-kari. They will also
buy and enjoy the gentle poems of the great Japanese
poet Basho (1644–1694) the superb master of the
*haikai* or seventeen-syllable poem. (The following one
is from the translation by Fosco Maraini.)

> *Behold! A camelia flower*
> *Split water when it fell!*

Basho's view of life, shared by so many other poets
and artists, might have been derived from a new and
tender offshoot of Buddhism, the cult of Buddha Amida
or "Unlimited Light" that preached charity and love.
The resemblance between Amida and Shinto are many:
simple ceremonies and not many of them. Like the
Quaker faith of the West.

The samurai and the lords they served looked for
spiritual guidance elsewhere, and found it in Zen Buddhism. One can imagine some armored lord shouting:
"Now there's a religion for soldiers . . ."

The Zen monks practiced a military discipline in
their monasteries and scorned books and the intellect.
Actually, they were heretics, for all Buddhists regarded
the Sutras, the sacred books of India, in the same way
as professing Christians regard the Holy Bible. They

expressed their heresy in a famous poem. (I quote the translation of Sir Charles Eliot.)

> *A special tradition outside the scriptures;*
> *Not to depend on books or letters:*
> *To point direct to the heart of man* . . .

If the Zen monks exalted "the heart of man" as the seat of powerful and primitive emotions, the artists influenced by Zen painted the heart of nature: the sea in its stormy fury but also in its magical calm. It must be admitted that the simplicity of Zen could only be beneficial to art. Zen values were adopted by other Buddhist cults. All Buddhist altars, for example, had been adorned with flowers. Zen preached that one single flower could be as soul-satisfying as a hundred. To this day, flower arrangement is an art in Japan, with a hundred different ways to show a single flower or a handful. Americans tend to fill up half a dozen vases, using flowers like a colored tapestry "to brighten up a room."

The Japanese have always been as delighted with flowers as little children. Even the most cruel of lords favored them as emblems, unlike the lords of medieval Europe who preferred lions, bears, and eagles on their crests.

But it was as lions and bears in human form that the shoguns governed Japan. Not until 1333 did any emperor attempt to restore imperial rule. When Go-Daigo, the King of Heaven, challenged the *bakufu* he was exiled to the island of Oki. Like a Japanese Napoleon he escaped, returning to Honshu in a fishing boat, hidden under heaps of seaweed. Go-Daigo's followers rallied behind the imperial flag of the Rising Sun. Kamakura fell and Go-Daigo declared that a new era had begun. It lasted for exactly two years as the plotters wove their silken webs. Betrayed by one of his trusted commanders, the emperor once again was exiled. For the rest of his life he lived in the hills of Yoshino as if on a second Oki.

The imperial rebellion, however, had exposed the weakness of Kamakura and the Kamakura men. The iron fist had rusted. Rival factions contended for power, and the Onin Civil War devastated the entire country from 1467 to 1477. The two hundred or so great lords devoured each other like a school of sharks. Pirates raided the coastal towns, bandits infested the mountains. It was an age of the sword. For two centuries Japan flamed with insurrections and disorders. The chronicles of the time all repeat the same tragic tale of fire and bloodshed, hunger and disease, of moneylenders grown swollen with wealth like vultures and samurai begging for coins. No one escaped. Even the lords perished. Only a dozen survived, the *daimyos*, which literally means "big names." Like independent princelings they divided the country into a dozen little kingdoms.

Central rule had vanished; chaos was enthroned. These were the years when Kyoto, the capital, burned to the ground, a smoking charnel house in which only forty thousand of its residents survived out of a population of half a million.

Three giant figures would soon appear to unify the nation. The first was Oda Nobunaga (1534–1582), a brilliant general with qualities similar to those of the legendary Yoritomo. Nobunaga crushed the daimyos and subdued the rebellious Buddhist monks of Mount Hiei. During his lifetime, the "southern barbarians," as the Japanese called the Portuguese, rowed ashore from their ships in 1542. A forever memorable date for the Japanese! After the Portuguese came the Spaniards, Dutchmen, and Britishers to establish trading posts and to preach Christianity. The new religion captured the imagination of a people who had always been susceptible to mystery. Some half million Japanese embraced the Cross of Christ, the Prince of Peace who like some celestial samurai had sacrificed his life, not for some heavenly daimyo, but for all who believed in Him.

Oda Nobunaga tolerated the new religion but in 1582 he was slain by a rebel general. His successor Hideyoshi had been a close friend but, unlike Nobunaga, his name to the Japanese Christians would soon be feared and hated as if he were the Devil himself. Hideyoshi's rise to power is unique in Japanese history. The son of a peasant, a stable boy with a knack for horses, he had followed his master into the civil wars. Before they ended, he had attained the rank of general in the armies of Nobunaga. Physically smaller even than most of his countrymen, Hideyoshi's ambitions were on a grandiose scale. As one of Nobunaga's closest advisers he proposed that Korea could be conquered, if he could have the ships. Where would the funds for an invasion fleet come from? Hideyoshi proposed that they use the taxes of Kyushu for one year. Once Korea was subdued, the combined Japanese-Korean armies would be free to attack China! Nobunaga smiled at these grandiose schemes but he valued his peasant-born general and rewarded him with the highest honors. Who but Hideyoshi could succeed the great Nobunaga as shogun?

And succeed him he did. He built the largest and most formidable castle in Japan at Osaka. Like the Popes in faraway Rome who commissioned the greatest painters and sculptors, Hideyoshi sought to outdo the most renowned art patrons of the past, even the emperor himself. Previously, brilliant color had been limited to book illustration. The walls of Hideyoshi's magnificent residence, "The Dwelling of Pleasure," like huge pages glowed with sapphire skies and emerald-green fields, the clouds tinted with gold. The chroniclers, inspired by all this opulence, ransacked their own imaginations to write of "golden dragons in the clouds."

The golden shogun Hideyoshi, more accurately, could have been described as an iron despot. His imperious will had tamed the fiercest daimyos; those who still resisted lost their heads. As for the militant Buddhists who so many times in Japanese history had challenged the emperor, Hideyoshi squeezed the soldier-monks like so many oranges, leaving only the pulp of a dry and formal religion. He distrusted Christianity, too, as a potentially subversive institution. It must be admitted that he had cause. European missionaries denounced the "false gods" of Japan; their more fanatical converts set fire to Buddhist temples and attacked Buddhist priests. Hideyoshi, infuriated by the reports he was receiving, began talking of the "snakes I have taken to my bosom." Anger led to persecution. Then, in 1597, Hideyoshi ordered the crucifixion of twenty Japanese Christians and six Franciscan monks.

When all Japan was in his tiny, doll-sized hand, ambitious as no other shogun before him, Hideyoshi resolved to conquer China. His expedition crossed the Korean "bridge" and was stopped. In the retreat Hideyoshi, "the Japanese Napoleon," perished.

An aristocrat, Tokugawa Iyeyasu (1542–1616), inherited the sword Hideyoshi had gripped so firmly. A general under both Hideyoshi and Oda Nobunaga, and a member of the famous Minamoto family, Iyeyasu was as ruthless as the peasant-born Hideyoshi. He suppressed the rebellious daimyos who opposed his accession to power, and in the last of many battles beheaded forty thousand of his enemies. He initiated anti-Christian laws more frightful than those of Hideyoshi. His policy of *sakoku* or exclusion closed Japan against all Christian nations. To guarantee power for his descendants, a year before his death he exterminated the children and relatives of Hideyoshi.

For two hundred and fifty years, Japan would be governed by a long line of Tokugawa shoguns. Military dictators, all of them, but their family crest might have been that of a family of poets or artists. It depicted no sword or castle or other symbol of strength but a simple and modest spray of hollyhock leaves.

# FIVE

# The Closed Gate

TOKUGAWA IYEYASU established his *bakufu* at a new site: present-day Tokyo or Yedo, as it was called during his reign. Fourteen of his descendants would succeed the ruthless general. The Tokugawa name would blaze down the centuries like burnished steel. The emperors, at Kyoto, were still revered like images, and like images they were powerless, nothing but glorified notaries who confirmed the Tokugawas in their offices at Yedo.

The first Tokugawa, like so many other despots in world history, maintained law and order, but it was a law and order of his own making. He rewarded the daimyos who had been loyal to him with the best lands. The daimyos of dubious loyalty and the surviving families of the executed rebels got the leavings. These were called *tozama daimyo,* which means "outside lords." And in fact they were *outside* the good graces of the all-powerful shogun. Repressive edicts circumscribed all their activities like an iron fence. They couldn't repair their castles, travel freely, or even marry without permission. The Tokugawa dynasty — 1603–1867 — governed a nation in which army discipline prevailed. Each Japanese had his place. Below the shogun were two hundred and sixty-two daimyos and their families. Below them, the samurai and their families who, it has been estimated, numbered about two million. Then, in descending order, the peasants, craftsmen, and traders; and at the bottom the eta or untouchables.

Japanese society had always been organized on dynastic lines. The emperors who had inherited the sacred symbols of authority from the semilegendary Jimmu were chosen from a whole cluster of noble families. Yet, as Kings of Heaven, they all felt themselves to be related. Blood relationship wasn't necessary, as it was in Europe. There, the crown prince succeeded his father, and if the throne were usurped, a new line of kings would govern.

The three generals, Oda Nobunaga, Hideyoshi, and Tokugawa Iyeyasu belonged to different families. Yet, to the Japanese way of thinking, they constituted one military dynasty. The Japanese idea was that the master of any skill, art, or trade would always find his true inheritors from among his most gifted apprentices. If a general had no son to inherit his sword, or if his son preferred poetry to war, even a stranger could continue the dynasty.

Japan was a web of dynasties of all kinds: musicians and actors, sculptors and artists, poets and scholars, tea masters and ship captains. There were royal dynasties and humble dynasties, all of them mustered like regiments behind the commanding general, so to speak: the shogun.

The daimyos had their lands and castles. The samurai had their privileges. No one enjoyed true individual freedom. The samurai was forbidden to work at any trade but, since the country was peaceful, the problem of morale confronted the shoguns. How could they maintain military pride and martial spirit in an army of "peacetime soldiers"? The solutions, if they could be called that, were effective if often savage. For example, if a peasant failed to show proper respect to a samurai he could be killed on the spot. The samurai would wipe his sword on the clothing of the slain man and walk off knowing that he was within his *rights*.

Tokugawa law hung like a storm cloud over land and people. Any transgression could mean death or imprisonment. Were the Japanese Christians a dangerous element in the state? The solution — like Hitler's "solution of  the Jewish problem" — was wholesale annihilation. Between 1615 and 1637, the converts were slaughtered. Only a few hundred survived, and Tokugawa Japan, like Hitler's Germany, no longer had a "problem." The Nazis, it will be recalled, had their own special phrase for extermination of the Jews: *Judenrein* or "pure of Jews." Tokugawa Japan, too, had been rendered "pure of Christians" and in order to keep it pure, the gates of Japan were locked in 1639 to keep out the world and all dangerous doctrines. Any foreigner who dared enter the country could be arrested and executed. Officials supervised the sole exception, the small and restricted Dutch trading station at Nagasaki. Dutch medical works were prized but any Western book that even mentioned Christianity was banned.

After four centuries of internal disorders and civil war, Japan knew peace, a peace created by the military dynasty of Oda Nobunaga, Hideyoshi, and Tokugawa Iyeyasu. By 1721, the population had increased to twenty-six million. And as always rice was the measure of any individual's importance. The little daimyos possessed lands that produced 10,000 koku of rice each year. (One koku is roughly five bushels.) The next highest rank of daimyo, the castle barons, had an income of between 100,000 and 300,000 koku. The great daimyos had 300,000 or more. Every rank of samurai received a fixed allowance of rice for himself and his family and servants. People, of course, didn't go shopping with baskets of rice but used coins; the gold rijo was worth one koku.

Peace brought prosperity. The despised artisans and traders, who once ranked lower than the peasants in their rice paddies, had enriched the nation. Buyers and sellers thronged the markets in the great cities of Kyoto, Osaka, and Nagasaki. With wealth all the arts flourished.

In the century before the rise of Oda Nobunaga, a Japanese artist, Kano Masanobu, had founded a school in which masters and apprentices painted like the Chinese. Another great artist, Tosa, and his followers, disdained the Chinese style, achieving their effects by a subtle and delicate use of line. Eventually, the two schools merged, and a second Kano dynasty dominated Japanese painting and illustration for three centuries. The Kano artists painted to please the rulers who believed, like Hitler and Stalin in the twentieth century, that art had to serve the state. The Tokugawa shoguns, however, permitted an unofficial art: the *ukiyo-e* or "pictures of the ephemeral world." An art of landscape and portraiture: actresses and geishas, famous sages and samurai. At first, the technique was simple. A woodcut would be carved and hand-painted colors applied to the black-and-white print. The next advance featured two- and three-color printing. By 1765 as many as fifteen colors could be printed on the same sheet.

It was a technique that attracted nonprofessional artists or "Sunday painters," as we might say: merchants with leisure, samurai who had no battles to fight. The professionals produced enduring works of art. Hokusai (1760–1849), the greatest of all the *ukiyo-e* printmakers, did some thirty thousand drawings during his lifetime. Despite his fame he lived like an ascetic monk. The landscape of his country fascinated him, the mountains and forests, Mount Fujiyama. His beautiful, delicate line would influence many Western artists. Hiroshige (1797–1858) was another great and sensitive painter and printmaker whose subjects every Japanese had seen: birds and flowers, snow and rain, the moon and moonlight.

The dramatic arts included the *Noh* theatre that had originated in the fourteenth century. Most of the two hundred and fifty existing Noh plays were written in the fifteenth century and employed the elegant court language of ancient Japan. They appealed to the nobles, the scholars, to all who treasured the past. The staging dispensed with all the usual theatrical trappings. The masked actors appeared on a platform twenty feet square, supported by four pillars, open on three sides, and roofed. It was as if the simple shrines of Shinto had been the model. The chorus stood at the right, the musicians in the rear, the back wall unadorned except for the painting of a pine tree, the symbol of youth and vigor; the total effect was almost sacred. The word *noh* means "ability" in Japanese. And every Noh play is a carefully rehearsed and polished performance that combines dialogue and song, music, and dance.

The Kabuki theatre, originating in the seventeenth century, could be described as a popularized form of Noh. Melodramatic rather than subtle, its actors using exotic makeup instead of masks as they re-enacted the stories of heroes and warriors, great loves and lost loves. Noh plays invoked the mysteries of human existence, the masked actors almost priestlike in their solemnity: a dramatization, in a sense, of the rites of Shinto.

The architecture, too, reflected the duality of the Japanese mind. There was the typical dwelling, simple and aesthetic, its interior divided by *shoji* or screens that slid into grooves. When needed, furniture was brought in at mealtime, bedding at night. Each important living-unit had an alcove for flowers and a few objects of art, with separate spaces for kitchen, tea-drinking, and bath. In utter contrast, the shoguns and great daimyos and their vassals lived in huge gaudy palaces with gilded columns, decorated lavishly in gold and silver. Today, at Nikko, the showy architecture of the Tokugawas attracts millions of Japanese and foreign tourists. The modern Japanese is history-minded but, like his Western contemporaries, many have abandoned simplicity as a way of life.

Tokugawa Japan had banned Western knowledge and science; the literature of discovery and invention: astronomy, biology, chemistry, physics, engineering, and industrial techniques. Western medicine alone had been permitted to "enter" Japan. The Japanese presses printed medical and legal tomes, dictionaries and guidebooks, fiction and poetry, adventure and pornography. The poets, perhaps in unconscious rebellion against the pomp and luxury of the daimyos, condensed their thoughts and emotions to write the miniature haiku: poems of seventeen syllables. With a minimum of words, disdaining ornate adjectives and decorative effects, they achieved, at their best, a poetry as pure as a little mountain stream. Basho (1644–1694), the great master of haiku, as well as the innumerable poets that would follow him, all seemed imbued by the belief that nothing in the world was permanent except change. Life could be beautiful, but alas! it was short. And inevitably the Land of Darkness, described in the earliest Japanese chronicles, awaited both shogun and peasant.

The shoguns dictated every aspect of Japanese life. They regulated the rights and privileges of daimyo and samurai. They valued the peasants who grew the rice and fed the nation, but never respected them. In the same manner, they valued the craftsmen who built their castles and fashioned their weapons. Below these — to use a Hitlerian phrase — were the "subhumans," the makers of nonmilitary things and objects, the merchants and traders, the moneylenders. The very clothes people wore indicated their positions in society. Even the way they arranged their hair was determined by the Tokugawas, who dictated the hairstyles of every class in the nation.

It is an irony of history that these dictatorial managers helped dig their own graves. Since they had forbidden the samurai to work, something had to be done to fill in the idle hours of their swordsmen. The shoguns encouraged the samurai to read Japanese history and literature. Learn from the past! The ancient chronicles written almost a thousand years ago, the *Kojiki* and *Nihon-shoki,* would undermine the loyalty of many thoughtful warriors. For these works documented the supremacy of the emperor. Who stood highest in Japan but the King of Heaven? And if this were so, what were the Tokugawas but usurpers? And when they read the ancient Shinto texts, many a samurai was reminded of the simplicity and austerity of their ancestors.

Yes, books have always been "dangerous" to tyrants.

In 1853, Commodore Perry's warships steamed into Tokyo Bay and the closed gate of Japan trembled as if shattered by cannon balls. It was the doom of the Tokugawas, the builders of the gate. Fifteen years later the last of the shoguns bowed out of history. Emperor Meiji, "the Enlightened," would write the newest page. Western science, Western customs, like a mighty broom swept away the dust of feudalism. A nation that had been organized like an ant heap — daimyo, samurai, peasant, craftsman — changed into a nation of political parties with a Constitution and a parliament, the Japanese Diet. There was religious as well as political liberty. Students went abroad to study, machines hummed in the new factories, trains hauled coal to the new furnaces. Within an incredibly short time the Japanese had made their second great leap into the world. A modern industry supplied the armaments for a Western-type army and navy.

The Japanese military defeated China in the last years of the nineteenth century and Tsarist Russia in the first years of the twentieth, demonstrating to an astonished world that the samurai sword of the Tokugawa hadn't been put aside like some antique. Rather it was redesigned and deadlier than ever.

# SIX

# Japan and China

NINETEENTH-CENTURY China had the biggest population in the world — four hundred million people —
but the soldiers of the Manchu emperors, as late as the
1840's, were still armed with the horn-and-sinew bows
of their ancestors. China had invented gunpowder but
it was the West that had perfected firearms.

The Manchu emperors, like the Tokugawa shoguns,
had attempted to isolate their realms from the West.
They restricted foreign trade to the one port of Canton.
This "closed door" policy infuriated the colonialists. At
first they attempted to unlock it without the use of
force with a key made out of opium.

The British doubled their opium trade with China
just as settlers in North America used whiskey or "fire-
water" as a weapon against the Indian tribes. In Can-

ton, the Manchu officials forbade the importation of the demoralizing drug. The British instantly retaliated. Their naval vessels bombarded the Cantonese forts and attacked the other port cities.

The Chinese fought with bows and axes and whatever muskets they had. Gongs rang in the coastal villages, summoning the people to resist the "foreign devils." British landing parties slaughtered the defenders. The outcome was inevitable. In 1842, the Manchu emperor signed a one-sided treaty with Britain, a document reducing a sovereign nation to inferior status.

The "century of shame," as the Chinese would describe it in their history books, had begun. Decade after decade, Britain and the other Western powers, Tsarist Russia and Japan, steadily enlarged their "spheres of influence" — a glossy diplomatic phrase that covered up the ugly truth of colonial exploitation. The Manchu rulers were helpless and in these years of crisis new leaders arose who sought to arouse "the sleeping giant," as the Western press had dubbed the vast and backward land.

Dr. Sun Yat-sen (1866–1925) had been born near Canton into a Christian Chinese family. A patriot, a student of history and politics, he founded the Society for the Revival of China. In order to survive, Dr. Sun declared, the nation had to be reborn as a democratic republic. He organized the many anti-imperial parties into a revolutionary league that would become the National People's Party or the Kuomintang.

Riots and armed uprisings undermined the dying Manchu dynasty. The emperor was forced to abdicate the Dragon Throne, and on January 1, 1912, Dr. Sun became the first president of the new Republic of China. Millions rejoiced but throughout the land there were powerful individuals who felt that their own opportunity had arrived. They derided the new Republic and mobilized the troops of their private armies. To avert civil war, Dr. Sun resigned, to be succeeded by Yuan Shih-k'ai, a high-ranking officer in the Manchu army, the first of the many strong men and warlords who would plunge China into civil war.

The Western nations and Tsarist Russia, like a wolf pack circling for the kill, had been watching developments in China. Japan, too, had kept a predatory eye wide open. The Land of the Rising Sun had already bitten off sizable pieces of Chinese territory in the Sino-Japanese War of 1894–1895. And when the First World War began in 1914, Japanese troops seized the German-held concessions. Since Japan had joined the Allies — Britain, France, and Tsarist Russia — against Germany and Austro-Hungary there were no objections. The fact that China, too, had joined the Allies apparently bothered nobody but the Chinese.

Centuries ago, Hideyoshi in his castle at Osaka had dreamed of the conquest of vast China. The First World War, to the new samurai, seemed like the perfect moment to grab all China. Who would or could interfere? The British, French, and Russians were far away, locked in a life-and-death struggle with Kaiser Wilhelm's armies. The Americans, revolted by the bloodshed in Europe, echoed the slogans of the pacifists: "Keep out of war!"

Tokyo presented Yuan Shih-k'ai with an ultimatum: the infamous "Twenty-One Demands." If accepted they would have made China another colony of Japan, no different than Korea. The Chinese strong man was ready to betray his people on condition that the Japanese install him as emperor. But like some oversized dose of poison, the Twenty-One Demands appalled even his own followers. They were rejected. Momentarily, China was saved.

When the First World War ended in 1918, the Chinese envoys at the Paris Peace Conference argued that the German concessions seized by the Japanese should be returned. The Western diplomats listened and then awarded the concessions to the Japanese. The United States alone did not participate in this treacherous diplomacy.

The Chinese protested. Huge demonstrations filled the avenues of Peking, Shanghai, Nanking, Canton, and the other large cities. Demonstrators broke the windows of Japanese-owned stores, and in their wrath chopped down cherry trees, the symbol of the Land of the Rising Sun.

If the Japanese generals seemed like latter-day Hideyoshis, planning war and conquest, another Japan, the Japan of the people, lived and worked and prayed as in olden times. Their emperor, in his somber orange robes that resembled the first colors of the rising sun, was still the high priest of all that was divine.

"Japan is a thing of beauty," the American reporter Lincoln Steffens observed on his way home from the Paris Peace Conference. "I had never imagined that any civilized country, any civilization could be as lovely as Japan. . . . That, I thought, is the way all civilized countries will look when every detail of their life is brought up into harmony with their culture. . . . The grace of the Japanese, in palaces, in shops, in the tea house of the Japanese dancing-girls. . . . I sailed away from Japan with such a sense of graceful perfection as no poem, no works of art, no city, state, or nation had ever given me before. . . ."

What had Steffens seen in the year 1918?

A nation where man and nature were indivisible. Was the weather uncertain? So it was, but the rain that poured down on the rice fields came from the kindly gods. Rice was life, the mud in the streets another manifestation of the natural world. Cheerfully, the Japanese wore high wooden clogs when they ventured out of doors. They liked rain as much as their cloud-wrapped mountains on whose peaks they had always built their holy shrines. The flowers they loved were duplicated on the kimonos of the women in silken blossom and petal. Long ago, both men and women had worn loose flowing robes and used the sleeves as pocketbooks. Now the men dressed in dark Western suits and carried briefcases like the businessmen of Paris or New York. But no Westerners conducted themselves so ceremoniously. Friends and acquaintances bowed to each other when they met.

No Western home had so simple a design. Made of wood without nails, the Japanese home like some outsized toy could be taken apart. It was sparsely furnished, uncluttered, lacking stuffed couches and chairs. In fact there were no chairs. People sat on the floor or *tatami,* a uniquely Japanese invention made out of rushes, two or three inches thick, inside a wooden frame covered by a mat sewn across the top. Naturally the mud and dirt of the streets weren't brought into the house. They removed their shoes before entering the door and bathed before the evening meal. There were no seven-course or even two-course dinners; no knives or forks. Everything, fish and meat and vegetables, had already been cut into bite-sized pieces before being placed on the table. They picked up the morsels with wooden eating sticks or *hashi*. When a child was a year and a half or two years old, he had already learned how to use them. He had also been taught to eat everything in his bowl. Food, too, deserved respect. To leave anything uneaten was a sin, an insult to the farmers who had labored in the fields, an affront to the sun and the rains and the gods.

Japanese gardens might have been miniatures of the groves and forests and mountains where the Shinto gods dwelled, to be cherished and protected from the elements. In the winter, the bushes were covered with straw, the trees propped up with crutches so they could withstand the fierce winds. The pine, the symbol of all that was desirable in life — youth, strength, longevity — was especially loved. Countless artists had drawn or painted the pine. They appeared in the color-prints, on jewel boxes and mirrors.

Lincoln Steffens, like Lafcadio Hearn and other Americans in Japan, had responded to the harmony of Japanese life. They had ignored its many inequalities. The Japanese woman, over the ages, had been reduced to a shadow of her husband. Long ago, before the great influx of Chinese civilization, they had been almost equal to men, according to authorities on Japanese society. Buddhism, however, regarded women as inferiors and forbade them to enter holy places. This prohibition spread to the Shinto shrines. The Confucian doctrines of obedience further degraded Japanese women; the home was her place, her duties limited to being a good wife and mother.

Steffens, however, as a great reporter, had sensed the ominous shape of things to come: the samurai sword that floated in the brilliant blue skies: "If there should be a war between Japan and the United States, I would surely pray that it might be a war without victory . . ." War with the United States? Unthinkable in 1918. Yet, no sensitive visitor could shut his eyes to the Japan on the other side of the garden wall. There stood the generals and the admirals who subscribed heart and soul to the military code of bygone centuries — the *bushido* or "way of the warrior," a code that exalted courage, discipline, and obedience. The Japanese word for all these obligations was *giri*. In opposition to *giri* was *ninjo* or human feeling: the two eternal antagonists that had always fascinated the Japanese. They clashed in folktale and Kabuki play, and in the movies so popular with the Japanese in the 1920's. In the years between the two world wars, *giri* always triumphed over *ninjo*. Today, after the Japanese defeat in the Second World War, after Hiroshima and the A-bomb, the movies of Japan still portray this basic conflict. But now *ninjo* is the victor.

China in the 1920's was like a paper house doomed

to be blown away by the first violent storm. The warlords had seized entire provinces, battling each other
or fighting the Kuomintang; their weapons were supplied by the Western nations and Japan who all had
their favorite "strong men."

The Russians alone had changed their policy in
China. The October Revolution of 1917 in Russia had
overthrown the Tsar. Lenin and the other Russian revolutionary leaders had condemned Tsarist colonialism
and voluntarily surrendered the Tsarist concessions and
"spheres of influence." Soviet weapons and funds
flowed to the Kuomintang commanders. Dr. Sun, although not a Communist, was grateful. He sent his
bright young men to Moscow to learn the techniques
of the revolution that had raised the red flag over the
world's largest nation. Among them was the man who
would succeed Dr. Sun as the leader of the Kuomintang
— Chiang Kai-shek.

Chiang Kai-shek had been born in 1886 into a land-
lord family, married the daughter of one of China's
richest families, and worked in a Shanghai bank. A
Chinese dictatorship of workers and peasants, similar to
the Soviet Russian one, had no appeal for a man of his
background. What interested him in Moscow was military science. He had been a cadet in a Japanese military
academy and served in the Japanese army: warfare was
his consuming passion.

But there were countless Chinese to whom the Soviet Union seemed like a road sign pointing to the future. Mao Tse-tung, the future leader of the People's Republic of China, had been born into a peasant family in 1893. Unlike most children of peasants he had managed to get an education. In Peking he had been a librarian, working for "a mouse's wages." He had read the works of Karl Marx and joined the Chinese Communist party.

Implacable enemies in the future, Chiang Kai-shek and Mao Tse-tung were allies in the 1920's against the warlords. Both wanted a unified China. Both welcomed the experienced Russian revolutionaries as advisers.

The thought of a second huge Communist state appalled the diplomats in London, Paris, Washington, and Tokyo. All of them prayed for a dissolution of the Kuomintang–Chinese Communist alliance; prayed, plotted, conspired. The Japanese agents in China tirelessly warned the Kuomintang leaders: "The Communists say they are against Nippon and this is true. But if they cut off our heads, your heads will follow into the basket."

By 1927, the Kuomintang armies led by Chiang Kai-shek had routed the Chinese warlords. The prize cities of Hankow, Nanking, and Shanghai, the greatest city in all China, flew the White Sun flag of the triumphant Kuomintang. China, at last, was unified. That same year Chiang turned against the Chinese Communists. His execution squads slew them in all the cities. Mao Tse-tung, in Shanghai at the time, fled for his life. His wife and sister had been killed, his cause seemingly drowned in blood.

Indestructible, the Chinese Communists. They established Chinese soviets like red islands in the middle of the Kuomintang sea, then lost them, only to reorganize in the far north.

"Death to the bandits!" the Kuomintang cried.

"Death to the Kuomintang, the running dogs of capitalism!" the Communists countered.

The Tokyo military looked on as civil war again raged in China. They hated the Chinese Communists and favored the Kuomintang as did the Western nations, but their ambitions were limitless: the conquest of China. The tutors of Emperor Hirohito, who had ascended the throne in 1926, were the two great heroes of the Russo-Japanese War of 1904–1905: Admiral Togo and General Nogi. But Hirohito, the grandson of Emperor Meiji, exercised very little power. Power was divided between the military and the "Five" of industry: Mitsui, Mitsubishi, Sumito, Yasuda, and Okura. Japan's destiny, to them, would only be fulfilled on the Asian continent.

Superpatriotic organizations such as the Black

Dragon Society agitated for an immediate invasion of China. The society's very name evoked age-old memories. The dragon was the oldest mythological creature in Japan, a dweller of the deeps. Japan, with its seas, lakes, and waterfalls, had always been "dragon country," so to speak. The Black Dragon Society prepared millions of Japanese for the great day when the Japanese dragon would swim across the narrow stretch of water that separated the home islands from the Chinese mainland.

North of Japanese-held Korea lay the great plain of Manchuria, a Japanese "sphere of influence." On September 18, 1931, an explosion on the Manchurian railroad near the city of Mukden (the Japanese had blown up one of their own trains) served as an excuse for the long-dreamed-of invasion.

There had been Japanese statesmen of peaceful or liberal tendencies who had opposed the new samurai. Those that weren't forced out of public life had paid dearly for their principles. Between the years 1918 to 1931, five Japanese prime ministers had been assassinated. The wine of militarism had intoxicated an entire nation.

Japanese secret agents, throughout all the little countries of Asia, had been paving the road for the march of armies.

"Asia for the Asiatics!" was their slogan, their argument, their promise of a future free of white colonialism.

And wasn't the subcontinent of India a part of Asia? In Delhi and Calcutta Japanese agents attended Buddhist ceremonies and piously spoke of the great debt they owed India, the great land where the living Buddha had preached so long ago and in whose doctrines so many Japanese believed.

"The United States should stay out of the Far East," the Tokyo propagandists declared boldly, "and permit Japan to maintain law and order!"

Japanese militarism was racist. But unlike the Nazis, who divided the white people into a master race of German "Aryans" and lesser races of "subhuman Jews" and "inferior Slavs," the Japanese preached a union of all Asiatics, yellow, brown, or black. All religions, the Japanese said, were equal. The Buddhism of India, China, and Japan; the Mohammedanism of Java; the Catholicism of the Philippines.

"Asia for the Asiatics!"

And after Asia?

"In order to conquer the world, Japan must conquer Europe and Asia; in order to conquer Europe and Asia, Japan must first conquer China."

These frank words were written by General and Prime Minister Tanaka in 1927. Tokyo had disavowed the notorious "Tanaka Memorial," as the statement was called, but only because the right moment for the invasion of China still hadn't come.

China, to the Western nations of the nineteenth century, had been simply another vast area to colonize, like India or Indochina, like Egypt and the Arab lands, or the African territories south of the Sahara Desert. To Japan, the conquest of China was a psychological compulsion. Their superpatriots might jeer at the "land of the half-deads" but deep in the Japanese mind there were other images: the memory of the Central Realm from which Japan had received the Buddhist religion, her written language, the arts of printing and silk-making, and so many other gifts that it would take a book to list them all.

The roar of Japanese warplanes over Manchuria *proved* the superiority of the Japanese, the superiority of military might.

Chiang Kai-shek, to the amazement of his people, ordered his Manchurian divisions to retreat from their positions, to offer no resistance. Without striking a blow at the invaders, he proclaimed that the first duty of the Kuomintang was "to exterminate the Red bandits."

The Japanese generals, Doihara, Itagaki, Ishihara, led their armies into Manchuria and in four days won the first of the undeclared wars of the twentieth century. The vast Manchurian plain, a half-million square miles in area, with its thirty million people, its cities of Harbin, Fushun, and Kirin, its iron and coal, soybeans and wheat, had been presented to Tokyo like a great plum on a lacquered tray.

The Western democracies, the United States, Britain, and France, denounced Japanese aggression but dared not interfere. The Great Depression of 1929 had, by 1931, deepened into a seemingly bottomless hole of breadlines and closed factories, hunger and unemployment, fear and despair.

Out of the hole as if winged like demons, the militarists of Japan and Italy and Germany proclaimed a new order: the totalitarian state. Mussolini in Rome, Hitler in Germany, their followers everywhere, preached the doctrine of Fascism triumphant. Democracy? "Democracy was weak and decadent!" the Fascists cried in chorus, and it would be wiped out like the plague of Communism!

On January 28, 1932, another Japanese army attacked Shanghai.

*"K'ang jih!"* Resist Japan! — these Chinese words were a prayer, an accusation, a cry of agony. In Shanghai, the Kuomintang Nineteenth Route Army fought heroically, without support from Nanking, the capital of Chiang Kai-shek. The Japanese soldiery looted, murdered, and raped to celebrate their victory. All China was horrified. Nevertheless, Nanking signed a peace

agreement with the Japanese, granting them the right to keep their troops in China's greatest city.

But there was no satisfying the Japanese military. In 1933 the armies in Manchuria, renamed Manchoukuo, moved southward into the northern Chinese provinces, encircling the cities of Peking and Tientsin. Again Nanking ordered nonresistance while the Tokyo generals tightened their siege. To Nanking, the chief business on hand was to crush the Chinese Communists. Its propagandists were tireless in denouncing the "Red vermin" even as they urged the Chinese people to treat Japan as "a friendly neighbor."

"When shall we bind fast the gray dragon?"

This plea of Mao Tse-tung, written in his northern stronghold, found an echo in tens of millions of Chinese hearts.

Gulping down what it had already seized, the gray dragon sprang at northern China. The dragon came by sea, by land, by air. It rode in huge tanks manufactured in Britain by the firm of Vickers, in convoys of trucks made in the United States by the Ford Company. Dutch gasoline powered the aerial armadas in the sky from which Japanese pilots and bombardiers prepared to drop French-made explosives.

The Western democracies had steadily condemned Japanese aggression in China. Yet, ignoring the protests of millions of their citizens, they continued to sell war goods to the aggressors. These were the years when Mussolini and Hitler had seized power in their two nations. Arrogant and confident, they promised their black-shirted and brown-shirted followers that the iron hand of Fascism would rid the world of both democracy and Communism. In every Western democracy, the native Fascists paraded, imitating their masters in Rome and Berlin. In every Western democracy there were statesmen, financiers, and industrialists as well as "little people" who feared Communism more than Fascism.

*Appeasement* was the ugly word heard in these fateful years. Heard again and again! The Western leaders stood silent when Loyalist Spain was "saved from Communism" by its rebellious Fascist generals. They were mute once again when Hitler's Brownshirts marched into Czechoslovakia, the only democratic republic in Central Europe.

In distant China, the Japanese high command issued the "Three-All Policy" in a final effort to crush the resistance of any man, Communist or Kuomintang, who still dared to fight: *"Burn all, kill all, loot all!"* Japanese bombers ignited countless Chinese villages and towns. Hordes of refugees poured into the cities, all telling the same story of fear and terror.

Appeasement was like a huge rubber band but at last it had to snap.

Just below the Great Wall of China, a powerful

Kuomintang force, the famous Tungpei Army, had besieged a Red army. The Tungpei were Manchurians whose homeland had been the first to vanish down the maw of the Japanese dragon. In their ranks first a few, then many, began to criticize the policies of Chiang Kaishek. "Let's aim our guns at the Japanese devils . . . Chinese must not fight Chinese . . ." The slogans were taken up by the entire army, officers and commanders as well as infantrymen.

Like some mighty shout it reached Nanking. Generalissimo Chiang hastily flew from his capital to confer with the Tungpei commanders. They swore their loyalty but insisted that they wanted to fight the Japanese. They dismissed Chiang's arguments about the need of first crushing the Reds. And then actually, without harming him, they held the Generalissimo as a prisoner. He was a pawn in a bizarre chess game played by three players: the Tungpei, the Kuomintang, and the Chinese Communists.

Within a month after the famous kidnapping, the Kuomintang and the Chinese Communists joined in a second united front that would last from 1937 to 1945. Again China was united, but ten years of civil war had drained its blood. Too weak to halt the mechanized divisions of the Rising Sun, Chiang in 1938 had to abandon Nanking, fleeing to Chungking, seven hundred and fifty miles in the interior.

The newly forged Kuomintang–Chinese Communist alliance was both a surprise and a challenge to the Japanese high command. Tokyo ordered its field commanders to wind up the war — as if victory could be ordered like any other commodity. The Japanese armies in China swept south of the Great Wall.

The Chinese forces retreated, on their lips a new song:

*Springtime — a hundred flowers unclasp their lips;*
*The Japanese devils have seized our land.*

The devils, armored in steel, forced the Chinese back to the Yellow River. No attempt was made to hold the northern shore. The Chinese only felt secure when they had ferried across the turbulent waters to the southern shore.

From ancient times, the mighty river had been known as "China's Sorrow," constantly overflowing its banks, drowning the villagers and ruining their crops. But like the Great Wall of China, the Yellow River had also been a barrier against the war hordes of northern Asia who throughout Chinese history had ridden south on their horses to trample the peoples of the Central Realm.

To the Japanese general Doihara, the conqueror of Manchuria, the Yellow River was simply an engineering problem easily solved. At night his advance units, in swift motor launches, crossed to the southern banks, wiping out the Chinese river garrisons. His planes machine-gunned every fortified point; his engineers constructed pontoon bridges. The iron machine Doihara commanded clanked and roared over the waves. And again the Chinese retreated, their movements reported by the Japanese observation balloons overhead.

The retreat almost became a rout as the peasants deserted their villages. People on foot, on bicycles, in donkey carts, blocked the Chinese army trucks. The Japanese only stopped when they outraced their supplies. The fleeing Chinese regiments regrouped. The Japanese gave way and slowly retreated back to the Yellow River.

At this crucial moment, "China's Sorrow" became the savior of China. Chinese engineers dynamited the earthen dikes, unleashing columns of rushing water which engulfed the Japanese, inundating the towns and driving millions from their homes. The Yellow River, out of control, fifteen miles wide at some points, divided China into two parts: the north held by the Japanese invaders, the south by the defenders.

Yet China's salvation was only temporary. By 1938 the Japanese controlled all the railroads and highways. Some of the Kuomintang armies fought bravely; others led by pro-Japanese generals seemed more interested in blockading the Communists. There were rumors that Chiang Kai-shek, and if not he, some of his closest advisers, had recommended a wait-and-see policy. Why antagonize all-conquering Japan who perhaps would win the final victory? The flag of the Rising Sun flew in all of the great cities. Neither the Kuomintang nor the Chinese Communist armies could retake them. But at night the Communist guerrillas recaptured the countryside. Led, as the guerrillas said, by "the general of night and darkness," they agitated among the peasants, recruited new Red Army soldiers, and predicted eventual victory.

Few Western observers in 1938 believed in these promises. It seemed as if "the century of shame" begun in 1842 by the British had finally been completed by the Japanese. Consummated, at last, the dream of the shogun Hideyoshi: the conquest of vast China.

# SEVEN

# "Remember Pearl Harbor"

$P$EARL HARBOR, so surprising at the time, was inevitable. Like so many of history's thunderbolts it burst out of the turmoil of an entire century.

Japan, victorious against Russia in the Russo-Japanese War at the beginning of the twentieth century, had become a world power. With each decade Japan grew stronger and more ambitious. In 1910 Korea was annexed. In 1915, during the First World War, the militarists in Tokyo proposed the grandiose Twenty-One Demands which would have reduced China to a Japanese protectorate. Great Britain and France opposed this plan. Temporarily, the samurai sword was sheathed, to be unsheathed again in the 1930's when the Japanese marched into China.

When the Second World War started, Japan signed a military alliance with Germany and Italy. Japan was now openly on the side of the "new men" — Hitler and Mussolini — whose announced aim was the destruction of the Western democracies and a new division of the world.

Tokyo created the Co-Prosperity Sphere that it was hoped would bring all Asia under Asiatic leadership. And these leaders, of course, would be the Japanese. From a military viewpoint, the United States air and naval bases on the Philippine Islands, five hundred miles off the coast of China, and due south of the Japanese islands — the steel center of the Co-Prosperity Sphere — had to be eliminated. Further out in the Pacific, the Hawaiian islands also were a threat to the Japanese expansionists who dreamed of dominating the entire ocean and of even raising the Rising Sun over Alaska and California.

The United States was huge and powerful. But the Japanese samurai, remembering how easily they had beaten the Russians in 1904–1905, began to coordinate their plans for a massive surprise attack in the Pacific. The Nazi slogan — Tomorrow the World — could have been the slogan of the samurai.

The thunderbolt that would be known as Pearl Harbor was readied for release.


No American would ever forget December 7, 1941, when the Japanese, in a two-hour raid, struck Pearl Harbor in Hawaii.

America's chief naval base in the Pacific, Pearl Harbor, guarded the Pacific Ocean states of Washington, Oregon, and California. With its flying fields and military installations it seemed impregnable.

The Japanese planes attacked at dawn — each painted with the symbol of the Rising Sun — at an hour full of associations for the Japanese throughout their history. They winged off their carriers — fighters, bombers, torpedo planes — to sink or damage eight American battleships and seven other war vessels. American planes burned on the ground.

"The attack . . . was in the Japanese tradition," Harold L. Ickes, secretary of the interior in President Franklin D. Roosevelt's cabinet, observed in his famous diary. "The late Admiral Togo, Japan's naval hero, did the precise thing — in 1903, I think it was — at Port Arthur when the Russian fleet was put out of action by a surprise attack. . . ."

For the overjoyed Japanese, Pearl Harbor was a promise of inevitable victory; for the stunned Americans, the beginning of a war whose outcome no man could foresee.

That same day of December 7, still other aerial fleets attacked the islands of Wake and Guam, and the Philippines. The air-raid sirens wailed in Manila, the Filipino capital, the church bells tolled as the Japanese planes like a flock of destructive silver birds dropped their deadly loads on the waterfront and on the flying fields at Camps Clark and Nichols. Billowing smoke lifted up from almost a hundred American planes burning on the ground. "Sitting ducks," as Americans would say afterward.

North of Manila, the troops of the Japanese Commander-in-Chief Homma disembarked from their landing craft to raise the flag of the Rising Sun on the island of Luzon, the main island in the Philippines chain.

It was *blitzkrieg* or "lightning war" that the German Nazi war machine had perfected to conquer all Europe except for the British Isles and Soviet Russia. By 1940 France and all the countries of Western Europe had fallen. Fascist Rumania, Hungary, and Bulgaria had collapsed without a bullet being fired. The Yugoslavs and the Greeks had resisted until they, too, were overwhelmed; their guerrillas alone continued to fight the Nazis. Hitler, the master of Europe, like Napoleon prepared to seize Moscow. True, he had signed a nonaggression treaty with Stalin and vowed friendship with his former Communist enemies. Stalin, to safeguard Soviet Asia, had signed a neutrality pact in April 1941 with Japan, Hitler's ally. "We both are Asiatics," Stalin had smiled at the Japanese ambassador. There was some truth in the statement, for Stalin had been born in Georgia, the age-old crossroads between West and East.

Nothing saved him. On June 22, 1941, the Nazi blitz like a sheet of lightning, a thousand miles wide, tore into Russia to scorch city and town and countryside, killing millions of Soviet troops and civilians.

Blitz war was a war of surprise, and of betrayal. For as the Japanese bombs fell on Pearl Harbor and Manila, Japanese representatives, proper diplomats in striped trousers, sat in Washington, D.C., talking peace with American officials.

*Filipinos, surrender*
*Our quarrel is with America*
*Not with you Filipinos*
*Who are our brothers in Asia*

Japanese leaflets such as the above followed the bombs, floating down to the streets of Manila, which had been declared an open city — a nonmilitary target — by the Filipino authorities. All fighting men, American or Filipino, had left the city, retreating to the peninsula of Bataan. Manila, defenseless, would fall to the Japanese on January 2.

That seventh day of December was a day of disaster for Americans and Filipinos. A day of glory for the Japanese in their home islands, and in the occupied cities of Asia: "In Tokyo, Shanghai, Peiping and many other cities," the Chinese novelist Lau Shaw wrote in his novel, *The Yellow Storm,* "the bloody mouths of the demons of war had long been ready at the microphone. As the planes neared Pearl Harbor, before a bomb had been dropped, the mouths had opened and spat out what had been prepared, 'the American Navy has been entirely destroyed.' The Japanese in Peiping were again delirious with joy. . . . Crowds upon crowds — carrying their wine bottles, mightily shouting, 'Great Japan, ten thousand years' — staggered through the streets, and jumped, and danced. They had defeated America, they were the lords of all humankind."

The Japanese attack aroused all America. It united the people, including the pacifists and isolationists who had hoped and prayed that America somehow might escape the worldwide conflagration ignited by the totalitarians in Asia and Europe. There were exceptions, of course: native Fascists like the Silver Shirts who had aped the Brown and Black Shirts of Hitler and Mussolini. There were sizable German-born and Italian-born elements whose hearts responded to the oratory of Berlin and Rome, as well as prominent "hundred-per-cent Americans" who like Chiang Kai-shek feared Communism more than Fascism.

On December 8, 1941, President Franklin D. Roosevelt addressed Congress and declared war against

Japan. Hitler summoned his puppet parliament, the Reichstag, in Berlin to accuse Roosevelt of being "a war maker and a gangster." And before he finished his demagogic speech he declared war against the United States.

The battle was joined in Europe, Asia, Africa — a struggle for the globe involving the far-flung continents and all their peoples. Hitler had his master plan, the "Thousand Year Reich," in which the "Aryan" race would reign supreme into the distant future. The Japanese leaders had their Co-Prosperity Sphere like a glittering bauble to dazzle the nations of Asia.

Both Nazis and samurai hated Communism and democracy. This was their rallying cry, their common platform and program. The United States and Britain, too, had feared Red Russia, but the Fascist blitz permitted no more reservations. For as the old American saying puts it: "When the house is burning you don't ask questions of the guy who hands you a pail of water."

During the years 1941–1943 the Germans and Japanese seemed invincible. Hitler's armies encircled Leningrad and marched to the gates of Moscow. The Japanese, on December 7, had seemingly delivered a fatal blow to the American Goliath.

In the Philippines the only remaining resistance was on Bataan and the island fortress of Corregidor, or "the

Rock." There, in the leech-infested jungle, and on Corregidor in the tropical sea, the American Filipino forces had dug in, waiting for help to arrive from America. It would never come. The Philippines were lost. General Douglas MacArthur, top-ranking officer, had flown from Bataan to distant Australia. There, plans were made that eventually would drive the Japanese out of the Philippine islands.

Bataan would go down in history as an epic of courage and a nightmare. "As for food," Colonel E. B. Miller, one of the survivors of the Japanese prison camps, wrote in his book *Bataan Uncensored,* "on entering Bataan on January 7th, orders greeted us that all troops would go on half-rations. By the end of February, we were visibly weakening. Morale and mental attitudes were of the best but physique was decaying rapidly . . ."

Bataan's defenders had slaughtered and eaten their last horses and mules. They were constantly being strafed by Japanese planes or else bombarded with leaflets. One of them pictured an American skeleton holding out for a lost and hopeless cause.

Nevertheless, they held out while the British bases at Hong Kong and Rangoon fell to the samurai. They held out after the great British naval base at Singapore and its seventy-five thousand defenders surrendered to

Japanese General Yamashita, nicknamed "the tiger of Malaya." And even when Bataan surrendered, the American flag flew on the Rock of Corregidor until May 6, 1942.

A month earlier, in April, sixteen American bombers had roared off the decks of the aircraft carrier, the U.S.S. *Hornet,* flying eight hundred miles to drop its bombs on Tokyo. The famous "Doolittle raid" did very little damage to the Japanese capital, but for the American people at home, working around the clock in war plants, it was a promise of eventual victory.

Remember Bataan! Guadalcanal! Iwo Jima!

Year after year these names out of the remote Pacific would echo across the United States where millions of men and women, in shipyards, factories, aviation and munition arsenals, had joined together to produce what would be a made-in-America blitz.

Asia for the Asiatics!

The Japanese had their own slogans and like explosives they had shattered the colonial empires of the British, French, and Dutch. In the Dutch East Indies, that vast archipelago of islands whose names for centuries, in the Western imagination, had rung like mysterious gongs — Java, Celebes, Sumatra — the Japanese had freed the political prisoners, the anti-imperialists and nationalists. Among them was Achmed Sukarno, destined to be the first president of the Republic of Indonesia, the fifth largest country in the world with a hundred million people.

"Cooperate with Nippon! Aren't we both Asiatics?"

The Japanese found numerous prominent Filipinos to collaborate with their generals and administrators. But many like José Abad Santo, chief justice of the Philippines Supreme Court, displayed the courage of legendary heroes. Santo defied his captors who condemned him to death. "This is a rare chance," he told his weeping son. "Not everyone is given the opportunity to die for his country."

Enlightened U.S. policies in the Philippines had won many friends. On Bataan, Filipino soldiers fought side by side with the Americans. Still other Filipinos would turn guerrillas, under the command of such American officers as Colonels Thorpe and Fertig, to harass the Japanese garrisons in the islands of Luzon and Mindanao. If the Japanese propagandists had won over many of the rice landlords on Luzon, the peasants sheltered the Communist- and Socialist-led guerrillas who called themselves the *Hukbalahap,* or "People's Army Against Japan." The tactics of the Huks were modeled after those of the Chinese Communist guerrillas.

In Indochina, the Japanese propaganda appealed to the nationalists who had hated their French masters.

But there were many who distrusted the Japanese slogan of "Asia for the Asiatics" whose names would become world-famous in the postwar period. Ho Chi Minh, the president of Communist North Vietnam, had lived as a young man in Paris, where in 1920 he had been one of the founders of the French Communist Party. When the Japanese occupied Indochina, Ho Chi Minh led the anti-Japanese Vietminh guerrillas. His forces cooperated with the U.S. agents of the Office of Strategic Services. After Japan's defeat in 1945, the French attempted to restore their old colonial position. The Vietminh fought the French for nine years, defeating them in 1954, when the United States assumed the French role.

Eighteen years have passed — 1954 to 1972 — the longest war in American history, the most divisive, the most immoral. Almost fifty thousand American soldiers have been killed. A dismaying, a disheartening figure when one asks the question: "Why did they die?" For the Vietnamese, North or South, Communist or anti-Communist, for the Cambodians and Laotians, the statistics of the killed, the wounded, and the homeless are inadequate to describe a war that has turned these small countries into a province of hell.

Gunnar Myrdal, the famous Swedish sociologist, has in this author's opinion summed up the man-made hell that is Vietnam: "To the Vietnamese people a Communist state, intent on preserving a maximum of independence from China, could hardly be a worse alternative than a prolongation of the misery they have suffered for the past twenty years. . . . To the people in the village and the paddy fields, the Americans coming in their helicopters and jet planes to spread fire and death are more than powerful strangers: they are 'white devils' — a concept with a long tradition in this part of the world."

It should be apparent that the Japanese slogan of "Asia for the Asiatics" was not buried with Japanese defeat. Like some armed specter it has arisen, found new flesh and bones, and new life.

While all Asia burned during the Second World War, the Japanese islands seemed like impregnable battleships lying at anchor in a safe port. No bombs fell out of the skies, no blood stained the roads or the streets. Joyous crowds in Tokyo (as we know from numerous eyewitnesses, Europeans and Japanese) gathered daily at the Niju-bashi, the bridge in front of Emperor Hirohito's palace, bowing their heads in homage: old Japanese war veterans who had fought in the Russo-Japanese War at the beginning of the century, schoolchildren and war workers, clerks and professors, all of them carrying little flags of the Rising Sun of Japan. At night, after the ritual bath and evening meal, the record players in many homes maintained the patriotic mood with such popular army songs as "Soldiers Leaving for the Front."

Victory!

The Japanese dragon had swallowed the American Philippines, British Malaya, French Indochina, and, still unsatisfied, reached one claw across the Pacific to the icy Aleutian Islands to menace Alaska and the northwestern states of Washington and Oregon. A second claw swooped south to sweltering New Guinea to threaten Australia.

The old tale of St. George and the dragon, however, would soon be retold again. But this time St. George would be riding an airplane across the blue skies of the Pacific. On June 5 and 6, 1942, American planes attacked and routed a powerful Japanese navy without a single shot fired from any surface vessel.

The Battle of Midway was a perfect name for this decisive engagement in the middle of the Pacific in which the Japanese hopes of victory foundered with their sunken ships; it was a turning point in the war. Four of Japan's most modern carriers with their crews and officers went down to the bottom of the sea.

Tokyo's propaganda chiefs tried to conceal the high casualty figures from the public. The wounded survivors of Midway were secreted in a naval hospital and guarded like prisoners. But the news leaked — and there would be worse to come.

On August 7, 1942, General MacArthur's forces, moving north from Australia, landed on Guadalcanal in the Solomon Islands.

Guadalcanal!

Kolombangara!

Munda!

Salamaua!

"Island-hopping," as the GI's and gobs and Marine leathernecks said as they traveled the long watery road that led to Tokyo.

In the Japanese capital, the all-powerful Premier Tojo refused to acknowledge the bad news from his field and naval commanders. His obliging assistants blue-penciled the reports and the premier, in turn, edited them still further before calling on the emperor.

But no blue pencil could cover up the Japanese setbacks in 1943. The Japanese bases in the Aleutians were retaken. American pilots shot down the planes carrying Admiral Yamamoto, the Japanese commander-in-chief of the Combined Fleet, and his staff officers while on an inspection tour. (To the Japanese, this calamity was as terrible as the loss of Admirals Nimitz and Halsey would have been to the American public.) Guam was recaptured by an American amphibious force. Challenged as never before, the Japanese navy attempted to stop the steady American advance across the Pacific.

The Battle of the Philippine Sea!

When accounts of this new defeat reached Japan, a shaken people flocked to the Buddhist temples and Shinto shrines in the tens of thousands to pray for help from the gods. Three more Japanese carriers had been scuttled by the Americans and four hundred planes downed; only forty had survived.

For the Americans, the watery road to Tokyo had been cleared up to the Philippines. By the autumn of 1944, MacArthur's troops had landed on Leyte. The Japanese high command resolved, once and for all, to destroy American sea power and by so doing bottle up the Americans on Leyte. Three Japanese fleets that included six plane carriers, seven battleships, and two brand-new 64,000-ton super dreadnoughts — the pride and hope of the Japanese navy — maneuvered against the Third Fleet of Admiral Halsey and the Seventh Fleet of Admiral Kinkaid who between them had twelve battleships and thirty-two plane carriers.

American air power won the Battle of Leyte Gulf.

From Leyte, MacArthur's troops steamed northward to Manila, the great port of Luzon Island. "We shall return!" the Americans had promised in 1941 before fleeing to Bataan and Corregidor. The battle for Manila raged month after month from November 1944 to February 5, 1945, when the American flag was hoisted over the reconquered Filipino capital.

"Don't the Japs know when they're licked?" the GI's asked.

Most of them had never heard of the Japanese military code — the *bushido* or "way of the warrior" — but in the streets of Manila they had seen decimated Japanese units launch final, desperate suicidal attacks, or banzai charges, rather than surrender. And in the burning houses, cornered Japanese had chosen to blow themselves up with hand grenades rather than wave the white flag.

Japan had been defeated in 1945 but the war went on. At Iwo Jima, thousands of American soldiers were killed or wounded before the final victory. For the Japanese high command, the loss of Iwo Jima, a vital air base in the western Pacific and the largest of the Volcano Islands, was still another disaster. The American advance never faltered. GI's and Marines, with naval support, swarmed ashore on Okinawa in the volcanic Ryukyu chain of islands — to be pinned down by deadly fire. Japanese suicide pilots — the *kamikaze,* so called in memory of the "divine wind" that had destroyed Kublai Khan's invading fleet in 1281 — crashed their bomb-laden planes on the American ships offshore.

The Japanese garrison on Okinawa had numbered a hundred and twenty thousand men. Only twenty thousand remained when organized resistance ended on June 21, 1945. They had lost in killed or wounded *five-sixths* of their total fighting strength, and had killed or wounded forty-eight thousand Americans. The statistics speak for themselves. And speak, too, of the samurai traditions of their ancestors.

Japan was doomed. The islands that had mounted one of the greatest military adventures in history were now, in the fourth year of the war, vulnerable themselves. Night and day, American planes bombed the Japanese dockyards, steelworks, aircraft factories, and munition arsenals. The aerial attacks widened to destroy the people who had produced the matériel of war. Incendiary raids put a torch to countless homes. (The Japanese Home Office, after the conclusion of hostilities, estimated that almost two and a half million homes had been completely destroyed; and that close to a quarter of a million men, women, and children had been killed.) And still the suicidal resistance continued.

On August 6, 1945, an atomic bomb was dropped on Hiroshima, an old castle city on Honshu Island. Three days later, a second atomic bomb fell on the city of Nagasaki. Three hundred and forty thousand people lived in Hiroshima; two hundred and fifty thousand people in Nagasaki.

Countless books and articles would be written about the mushroom clouds, the radiation, the terror and horror that had come from the skies. Two-thirds of

Hiroshima's population was killed or wounded; one-third of Nagasaki's population was killed or wounded. The survivors would never forget the *pikadon* or "flash-boom" of the newest weapons man had wrought to destroy his enemies. And who knows? Perhaps, man himself . . .

# EIGHT

# Occupation

THE TWO ATOMIC BOMBS that fell on Hiroshima and Nagasaki snapped the sword of the samurai.

The Japanese press all struck the same funereal note: THE MOST TERRIBLE CRISIS IN JAPANESE HISTORY . . . THE NATION IS AT ITS LAST STAND . . .

Yet, when Emperor Hirohito acknowledged defeat, the people reacted as if a third atomic bomb had struck them. In their thousands, they marched to the imperial palace, kneeling and begging forgiveness of the King of Heaven. If only they had fought harder, worked harder, sacrificed more, if only . . .

Many important officials such as War Minister Anami committed suicide to expiate their sins and shortcomings.

On August 14, 1945, President Harry S Truman informed the American people of Japan's unconditional surrender. On September 2, the Japanese signed the formal documents on the battleship U.S.S. *Missouri* anchored in Tokyo Bay. President Truman had been born in the state of Missouri and this final scene had all the elements of a Greek drama. For it was the man from Missouri who had authorized the use of atomic bombs as weapons of warfare. They were the second and third to be manufactured in the world; the first had been tested — exploded! — in a desert of New Mexico.

Emperor Hirohito, too, had played a fateful role in this drama of warring nations. He had told his people to welcome their conquerors and his people obeyed. The decision not to remove him from the imperial throne had been a wise one. To the Japanese, Hirohito — the grandson of Emperor Meiji who had led his nation into the modern world — was the living symbol of two thousand years of history. He was the descendant of the long line of Kings of Heaven that went back to the first legendary Emperor Jimmu.

His position in Japanese society was unique as Ruth Benedict's book, *The Chrysanthemum and the Sword* — the guide for American policy makers — had clearly stated.

The first American soldiers landed in Japan on August 28, two weeks after their President's victory announcement. They were met by a stunned people who feared robbery, murder, and the rape of their womenfolk. For years, the Japanese propagandists had been beating the scare-drums of hate, depicting the Americans as huge white brutes, as red-faced devils with cow eyes. What else could they be? Who else but a breed of military monsters could conquer the unconquerable Japanese?

Never in all their history had the Japanese ever seen foreign troops in their cities.

The Americans stared at the crowds, silent and impassive, like so many porcelain dolls. They, too, distrusted the Japanese. They remembered all too vividly how the Japanese soldiery had fought on Iwo Jima and Okinawa, and in the streets of Manila. Memories of buddies killed or wounded haunted the minds of the American soldiers.

"We'll be shot at," the GI's whispered. "We'll be knifed . . . poisoned . . ."

But as the first weeks of the occupation passed there were no incidents. When General Douglas MacArthur stepped out of his car with its five-star pennant denoting his rank as a five-star general, the Japanese cheered and applauded as he walked to the door of his Tokyo headquarters. They seemed like the most peaceful people on earth, as if some other race of islanders had brought sword and flame to Asia. The gaping GI's shook their heads, utterly baffled.

"You just can't understand the Japanese," they said. But there were Americans who did understand. Ruth Benedict, for example, who had never set foot in Japan.

Defeated, occupied, their militarists discredited, their sons buried on every island in the Pacific, their children burned alive in the American incendiary raids, their cities devastated (except for Kyoto, spared because of its historical and religious significance) only the emperor and the emperor alone represented continuity. He was the sun in human form, the promise of a new day, the new Japan that had forsworn war and warmaking. Forever!

Men came and went. The fifteen Tokugawa shoguns had had their day like so many other powerful families. Only the emperor remained.

So now they were governed by "the blue-eyed shogun," as the Japanese called MacArthur . . .

MacArthur's regal presence, his flash and glamour, appealed to a people whose Noh and Kabuki drama celebrated so many heroic samurai and princely generals.

As it happened, I myself witnessed the respectful and sometimes even humble behavior of the Japanese when MacArthur stepped out of his staff car. I was the historian on the U.S. Mission to the Philippines and I had flown to Tokyo from Manila with other Mission members. Our chief, Paul V. McNutt, was U.S. High Commissioner to the Philippines and he had come to confer with General MacArthur. McNutt's responsibility was to help prepare the Philippines for independence — and on July 4, 1946, the Republic of the Philippines would become an independent nation.

"Mt. Fujiyama," I wrote in my diary, "seemed like a great big ice cream sundae in the sky as seen from our C-54. We landed at Asugi airfield and the procession of staff cars jolted towards Yokohama and Tokyo. We were forty miles from the capital. We passed bombed factories, lopsided shells of houses. The countryside was alive with Japanese on foot, on bikes, pulling carts. Autos chugged by powered by charcoal or alcohol for there was no gasoline. The first impression of the twentieth century in the Orient — the nose masks so many people wore against colds. Women in kimonos, babies on their backs like papooses, wearing the white nose masks. . . ."

Brilliantly colored kimonos and surgical-white nose masks — I was impressed by this fusion of East and West. But at the time — a cold shivery day in November 1945 — I knew nothing about the age-old Japanese habits of personal cleanliness that had impressed the first Chinese visitors in the second and third centuries after the birth of Christ. Who but a people who practiced so many rites of purification would be concerned with not spreading the germs of influenza?

Later that first day in Tokyo I went walking on the Ginza, the main business street, with Major Johnson, the pilot of our C-54. We bought a few souvenirs and had our portraits painted on silk in a department store. The Japanese artist, wearing a Japanese army cap, worked with incredible speed. When the colors dried we looked at the two huge ruddy faces he had drawn, each with eyes as round as those of a cow or a dog.

"We don't look alike," Johnson said. "That guy made us look alike."

So he did. To these slant-eyed, slight people, all whites looked identical. An attitude and a prejudice shared by innumerable Americans who claimed that they couldn't tell one Japanese from another.

A memorable day. We wandered through bombed streets that we scarcely noticed, for we had become too accustomed to the devastation in Manila: the same roofless buildings, the same staircases that led nowhere, the same piles of rock and rubble. We visited the Japanese Diet, glanced in at the Upper Chamber at rows of blue, velvet-backed chairs on which the four hundred and sixty-six peers of the defeated empire had sat under a dome of Japanese oak. Empty, and empty the gold and red velvet chair of the emperor with its Imperial Chrysanthemum.

Out on the street, the sidewalk black marketeers sold their shoddy or stolen wares. Pure cotton goods, as I would learn later, commanded a top price, and therefore any article of first-class quality would be described in the postwar argot as "a hammer of pure cotton." Or, "a cup of pure cotton."

That same week all of us on the McNutt mission did some sightseeing from the air. Below our C-54, we looked down at the Inland Sea, at mountains, rivers, pines, patches of green frozen ice that I had only seen before in Japanese color prints. But none of us had ever flown over a city shattered by an atomic bomb.

A city? This wasteland empty as any desert? It was only when we flew away from "the bull's eye" where the bomb had exploded that we could tell this indeed had been a city. The mysterious jutting stone fragments below? What were they? Remnants of walls perhaps? Further away there were recognizable walls or rather portions of walls. Still further away were occasional buildings, not intact, but as if the wreckers had come and departed without quite finishing their job.

Hiroshima!

All of us in that C-54 shared the same thoughts: one single thought. Yet, we came from every part of the country — U.S. High Commissioner McNutt from Indiana; Admiral Stockton from Florida; Major Johnson from Kansas. Our ranks, backgrounds, and ages were widely different, but all of us felt that there couldn't ever be another war. Impossible! Yes, impossible.

The memory lingered when we returned to Manila. For some of us, I'm sure, the memory of Hiroshima would linger for the rest of our lives.

Relations between conquerors and conquered, for many months, remained good. But even in the beginning, as in all occupations, the black marketeers and get-rich-quick boys had sprung up to fill the gap between foreign buyers and native sellers. Hundreds, thousands, tens of thousands of shady Japanese had one consuming passion: the American dollar. They sold souvenirs, war trophies, Rising Sun flags, jewelry, furs, and a hundred other objects.

Women, too, were for sale. Brothels encircled the American camps. And for countless GI's, the word *geisha* became another way of saying prostitute. Prostitutes there were but they had another name and it wasn't geisha.

Like the samurai, the geisha was a product of a society whose customs and lifeways had their own special history. Century after century, the Japanese husband had secluded his womenfolk. When a Japanese man entertained his friends or relatives they would go out together — no women! — to a restaurant or visit a tea-house or inn where the geishas provided the entertainment. They sang and danced and played musical instruments. As children, the geishas had attended schools similar — to stretch the comparison to the breaking point — to our schools of the performing arts. They could be compared to our movie starlets when they graduated, destined for a life of public entertainment and glamour. Like movie starlets, many geishas married rich and powerful men; others became the mistresses of such men.

The average GI or officer never understood or bothered to understand the customs of a people whom he distrusted or despised as war enemies or else dismissed with a shrug: "They're Japs, see. And all this stuff about East is East and West is West is goddamn true!"

The American occupation ended in 1951. General MacArthur left Tokyo. Gone "the blue-eyed shogun," still another page had been turned in Japanese history. Once more people began to go to the bridge before the imperial palace to pay their respects to Emperor Hirohito.

# NINE

# Resurrection

THE "DIVINITY" of Emperor Hirohito was officially abolished on September 2, 1945. Just the same, to the Japanese people he represented past, present, and future.

From ancient times the Japanese have felt human existence to be an unending process: a circle in which beginnings became endings, and endings beginnings. Every morning the life-giving sun, an orange circle in the sky, tinted the sea with the colors of the robes worn by the emperor on state occasions, and shone on rice paddies and gardens. Its symbol was the chrysanthemum. Chrysanthemum Day on September 9 was one of the great national holidays. The Imperial Chrysanthemum was sixteen-petaled and made of gold, the symbol of two thousand years of history. Of continuity.

As plants need sunlight, the Japanese needed their

emperor. Countless soldiers had gone to their deaths in the belief that "to die for the emperor is to live forever."

The Japanese measured the passage of time by the reigns of their emperors. Hirohito, the one hundred and twenty-fourth King of Heaven, had ascended the throne in 1926 to begin a new era, Showa 1. As of 1971, he has reigned forty-five years or Showa 45. When he dies a new era will begin.

In 1945 Hirohito had told his people to welcome their conquerors. They obeyed. Ten years later they had restored the empire. Today, Japan after the United States and the Soviet Union is the world's third strongest economic power. The 1970's may well be, as so many Western economists have predicted, the Japanese decade. Certainly Japan's phenomenal resurrection is a dazzling fact. In 1945 every major city except Kyoto had been blasted by the fire descending from the skies. All of them have been rebuilt — Tokyo, Yokohama, Osaka, Kobe, Hiroshima, Nagasaki — all are uglier and even more garish than in the prewar years.

The Japanese have always been indifferent about the looks of their cities. To the Japanese, the city is a thing to be used, a place to work, a vast complex of roads and buildings that belongs to everybody and nobody. Beauty is private. Even in Kyoto, its architectural gems like the Temple of the Celestial Dragon are either hidden behind walls or in secluded groves. Kyoto like

Rome is a museum city of palaces, temples, and shrines. The avenues of Rome lead to spectacular fountains, squares, churches, and pre-Christian monuments like the Coliseum. The avenues of Kyoto and all the other Japanese cities — disfigured by huge advertising signs and exposed electric power posts — seem to lead to factories and plants.

No other people so value their privacy; the Japanese home is almost a shrine. Before entering, the members of a family remove their shoes. To bring in the dirt and filth of the anonymous streets is unthinkable, a disgusting Western custom. It is as unthinkable as having the toilet in the same room as the bathtub. Before the evening meal the Japanese, like their ancestors, wash away the grime of factory and office, and once clean will step into the tub. This, as I have mentioned, is usually made of unpainted wood. To the Japanese there is no more beautiful or natural material. True, a great many people have gone "modern" and in countless homes chrome, plastic, and stainless steel have replaced wooden tubs and furniture.

In fact, the red sun on the national flag could be replaced by the emblem of a factory. As in all industrial societies, the cities have boomed, the countryside has lost and is losing its population. In 1945, one out of every two Japanese worked on a farm. Improved agricultural techniques have reduced this percentage to one out of five.

The heavy migration to the cities has inevitably aggravated the housing problem. Two million families, according to a recent survey, live in one-room flats, packed together like ants in cheap wooden structures, overshadowed by high-rise apartments and office buildings. The flat-dwellers of these dark urban valleys have demanded "the right to sunlight!" It is a slogan to be expected from a people whose supreme deity has always been the sun goddess Amaterasu.

Middle-income families cannot afford to build or rent a decent house within easy reach of the urban centers. There are thousands of applications for every available apartment in the government projects. Three rooms and a kitchen in one of them will cost eighty dollars a month; under private ownership the same apartment will rent for one hundred and eighty dollars.

The one-room flats rent for twenty dollars a month and will have a television set, a washing machine, and refrigeration. There is practically no unemployment, no "belt-tightening." Husband and wife between them will earn about three hundred dollars a month.

The monetary unit is the yen (in Chinese, *yuan* or "round piece") and it is the equivalent of 0.003 percent of an American dollar.

The average annual income has tripled in the ten years between 1960 and 1970. The government could truthfully declare in its White Paper on economic affairs that, "The people of Japan are living a considerably richer life materially today due to the remarkable expansion of the national economy."

Japanese industrial expertise is tremendous. Despite shipping costs, Japanese exports — the biggest factor in the country's phenomenal growth — undersell the world. Cotton textiles and silks, drugs and detergents, plywood and plastics, stainless steel and petrochemicals: whatever the product is, a radio or a ship, the Japanese can produce it for less.

Japanese textiles dominate the world market. Yet cotton and wool must be imported. Nevertheless, the finished goods will cost less than American textiles when put on sale in American stores. This is a staggering fact when we consider that the United States produces its own cotton and wool, and weaves them in mills close to the home markets.

"The Japanese work for less," complain embittered Americans in the textile industry, both management and labor. "They haven't got our standard of living. We've got to impose import quotas."

The pressure to impose restrictions, to keep Japanese goods out, is mounting steadily in the United States and in other Western nations. U.S. trade with Japan, the largest between any two nations, amounts to some eight billion dollars a year. The Japanese buy our cotton, coal, lumber, and soybeans, and sell us manufactured products. American businessmen ask: "Are we a colony? If they can make a thing themselves they'll keep our manufactures out with their high tariffs and taxes." The Japanese will buy five thousand American automobiles, for example, while selling close to three hundred thousand Toyotas and Datsuns in the United States.

Japan's huge global trade, carried in one of the world's greatest merchant navies, has brought the flag of the Rising Sun to every port. In the last fifteen years Japanese exports have increased 600 *percent.* No other people can rival the Japanese genius for merchandising. The Ministry of International Trade and Industry is famous for its in-depth planning, and its caution. The decision to compete for the world market in low-priced automobiles — to challenge the German Volkswagen — came only after long years of research.

When the Australians, too, began to talk of being a "colony," the Japanese quieted the Aussie critics by a new policy of investments. Formerly, the Japanese had purchased 50 percent of her bauxite, 40 percent of her coking coal, and 28 percent of her iron-ore requirement from Australia. Today the two countries, bitter enemies in the Second World War, have become partners in numerous mining projects built by the Japanese in Australia.

Japanese trade with her great Asiatic neighbors increases every year. The Japanese islands are specks compared to vast China with its 750,000,000 people, India with its 550,000,000 people, Indonesia with its 122,000,000 people. But the specks are covered with factories and plants, and the 103,000,000 Japanese constitute one of the world's most efficient labor forces.

That is why Western economists have propounded the question: "Will the twenty-first century belong to Japan as the twentieth to the United States and the nineteeth to Britain?"

When Emperor Hirohito officially opened at Osaka the first world fair ever to be held in Asia — Expo '70 — millions of Japanese rejoiced at the great honor. The fair guides pointed out the moving air-conditioned sidewalks, the computerized lost-child center, and all the other proofs of Japanese expertise. More thoughtful visitors were impressed by the Shinto priests who conducted purification rites whose origins had been lost in time.

Purification?

These cleanly people had fouled their coastal waters and Inland Sea, and filled their skies with noxious, manmade clouds.

A Westerner — Howard F. Van Zandt, the senior

officer in Japan for the International Telephone and Telegraphic Corporation — spoke for the Japanese themselves when, in a *New York Times* news story, he said: "Do we [the Japanese] want to be the richest country on earth, if in so doing our nation becomes the most polluted?"

The Japanese have come to still another crossroads in their long history, leading to a future no man can predict. Their capital, Tokyo, is the microcosm of an entire nation; the greatest city in the world, many visitors say, and certainly the greatest center of population. Tokyo Metropolis, as the Japanese call their capital, includes the twenty-three wards of the city proper with a population of 8,800,000. There is also the Saitama belt of surrounding towns and villages where another 2,400,000 Japanese live. This amounts to more than eleven million human beings or about one-tenth of the total Japanese population.

Tokyo Metropolis is the greatest urban complex in the entire world: a conglomerate of past and present, culture and industry, pleasure and work. At the center there is the old city with the imperial palace behind walls of huge irregular blocks, the top row covered with soil in which pines are rooted like silent sentinels. Frogs croak in the moats and it is hard to believe that beyond them, and in all directions, there are a score of other Tokyos: the waterfront with its docks and ships; the steel furnaces and oil refineries; the enclaves of business and wealth; the lecture halls and laboratories of the universities; the underground city of subways; the shrines and temples of Shinto and Buddhism; the nighttime city of pleasure.

If the gods of industry have joined the Japanese pantheon, the old gods still maintain their hold. Inari, goddess of rice, continues to be honored on three solemn days every year — when the rice is sown in the spring, when offerings are presented to the gods, and again in the fall when the emperor and people taste of the new harvest. On April 8, the birth of Buddha is celebrated by processions of solemn priests, the holy statues dipped in sweet tea. There are little shrines to some god or other on almost every street; especially popular is Jizo, the protector of children. In August Buddhist monks travel down the River Suma to pray for the drowned and to apologize to the fish of the sea for taking their lives. Like the American Plains Indians who begged forgiveness of the buffalo they slew in order to live, the Japanese have never forgotten the unity of nature in which man and fish and even the inanimate stones form one mystical fellowship.

And yet the same people, like the peoples of the West, have polluted their waters with industrial wastes and sewage, their fish and lobsters flavored (to use this culinary expression ironically) with such deadly poisons as mercury.

And like Westerners, the Japanese avert their eyes from the troublesome future when they go out at night. Nighttime Tokyo outdazzles New York City's Great White Way. The blinking squares and whirling circles of neon and electricity, the multicolored ideograms seem to say: forget the daytime, forget job and worry and all obligations and duties. Not too long ago, nighttime Tokyo was almost exclusively a man's world of restaurants, teahouses, theatres, movies, strip joints. Today, Japanese women and girls, in greater and greater numbers, have broken the tradition of centuries.

Are the seas polluted? No other country has so many specialized seafood restaurants. Some serve shark fins, others carp, eels, prawns, or *sushi* — raw fish. The *kamaboko,* a white fish topped with a seaweed called *nori,* is as popular as the hot dog of America. A soup of dried seaweed and fish flakes — *ichibandasho* — rivals our tomato soup. Every day six hundred and fifty tons of fish — compared to a hundred and twenty-five tons of meat — will be consumed. And as the Japanese eat their favorite fish dish, many a diner will undoubtedly sigh and talk of the good old days when the seas were clean.

Pollution was the big issue in the April 1971 race for the governor of Metropolis Tokyo, although the two contenders espoused very different politics. If Minobe attacked "militarism and fascism" while praising "peace and democracy," and Hatano attacked "Marxism-Leninism," both candidates supported huge anti-pollution and urban-development programs. Minobe, supported by the Socialists and Communists, proposed the expenditure of *fifty-two billion dollars* to clean up Tokyo and its waters. Hatano, representing the Liberals and Democrats (the party with comfortable majorities in both houses of the Japanese Diet) proposed a more modest expenditure of *eleven billion dollars.* And both candidates in an age of entertainment wooed the voters with music and dancing beauties and hoopla. So much so that the Japanese press described the race for governor as a "feeling campaign." Minobe won.

The Ginza, where once tens of thousands of American GI's had "killed time," has been described by visiting Westerners as "ugly . . . fascinating . . . tawdry . . . dynamic . . ." Countless billboards and signs strike the eye with the impact of psychedelic colors. Balloons advertising television sets and toothpaste, automobiles and accident insurance, float above the rooftops in a sky no longer the brilliant blue remembered by the older generation. It reminds the American tourists of their own cities: "The smog makes you feel at home . . . And the traffic . . ."

Honking horns! Gas fumes, smells of roast tea, perfumes! Crowds of shoppers that seem to have come off an unending conveyor belt. Sidewalk vendors and huge department stores. Like some department store itself, the giant city has something for everybody.

The Tokyo underground of subways with its shopping centers and promenades could be some preview of the future when an overpopulated globe may be forced to burrow beneath the surface for living space. The Yaesu, glittering with light, has three hundred and fifty shops that sell everything from rice to jewels.

Buy! Buy! Buy!

Cynical observers of modern Japan have declared that the Japanese live to work, and work in order to buy. The same thing could be said of all peoples. All of us want goods, commodities, gadgets, luxuries. And all of us cherish values not for sale in the marketplace.

Japan has the highest literacy rate in the world. Almost every city block has a bookshop. Everybody reads. Clerks, workers, housewives, students in their school uniforms. According to Donald Keene, the American writer and authority on Japanese literature, books are almost a necessity to the Japanese because as a people they have "an exaggerated respect for culture which is a heritage of the past." They read their own great writers, Kafu Nagai, Naoya Shiga, and the many other Japanese who entered world literature before the First World War, as well as the brilliant generation who began to write after the Second World War. It is interesting to note that Japanese literature only withered away during the years of military glory in the 1930's and 1940's. And they read the leading writers, too, of the United States, Russia, and Europe.

There are almost nine hundred universities in Japan with a total enrollment of 1,750,000 students. Seventy-eight universities are located in Tokyo, including such prestige institutions as Waseda or Meiji, named after Emperor Meiji, "the Enlightened." During the reign of Meiji, Western learning was absorbed with a passion unique in the nonwhite world. Japanese scientists have contributed to world knowledge. No one is surprised any more when some Japanese physicist or biologist is awarded a Nobel Prize.

Nevertheless, the Japanese are not Westerners. The duality of the Japanese mind and imagination can be seen in all their activities. Their sports include archery, fencing, judo, and karate — as well as track and *yaku* or baseball. The Noh and Kabuki theatres continue to attract large audiences — as do the avant-garde plays of the West by such writers as Ionesco, Beckett, and Brecht. An example of this duality can be seen in New York City where a sculpture by Masayuku Nagare, a student of Zen Buddhism and Shinto, dominates the plaza of the World Trade Center. It is the largest stone carving in modern times, made of black granite, thirty-four feet long, seventeen feet wide, fourteen feet high. Its two asymmetrical parts are divided by what might be a dry creek bed. The mirror-bright granite draws the sunlight down into the plaza. Abstract art, yes, but the work could be a monument to the Japanese sun goddess.

No other people are such devoted moviegoers. The Japanese film industry is the only one in the world completely supported by the home audience. In the United States, the respectables stayed away when the first movie houses were opened. In Japan, Emperor Meiji's son and heir, the father of Hirohito, attended the first Vitascope showing. American films have always been notable for swift action, European film for character portrayal. Japanese films show man *and* his surroundings as an extension of man himself.

The Japanese movie is usually realistic, depicting life as it is and not as it might be. It pictures the conflicts between the generations, between men and women, the rich and the poor. Increasingly, it is a movie of crisis in which a single actor — faceless and all-powerful, The Machine — confronts the human characters, and all too often molds their destinies.

Americans and Russians, Japanese and Chinese, no matter how different their societies, share one thing in common: the knowledge that has created the super-machines of this century. It is a knowledge that if uncontrolled could destroy man and his world. For a long time, thoughtful men have warned mankind of its Frankensteins: the man-made monsters of science and technology.

Paul Valéry, the French philosopher, in his book *History and Politics* describes a conversation he had in the year 1895 with a Chinese scholar:

"Nippon is making war on us." (The Chinese scholar declares.) "Her great white ships steam through our nightmares. They will trouble our estuaries. They will set fire in the peaceful night."

"They are very strong. They are imitating us."

"You are children," said the Chinese. "I know that Europe of yours . . ."

A Europe of smoking factory chimneys, of clanging armament works, of marching men in uniform, who would soon slaughter each other in the First World War.

The Japan that built the "great white ships" so long ago, in another generation would loose a metal storm on Asia. And today, if she so desired, could produce atomic weapons.

# TEN

# The Next Great Leap

JAPAN HAS ALWAYS had an amazing capacity to absorb new ways. Long ago, like a bright eager student seated at the foot of a sage, Japan learned all that ancient China had to teach. In 1868, under the rule of Emperor Meiji, the great leap to the West transformed a feudal nation. The Japanese flag, unknown on the seas of the world, flew from the staffs of one of the greatest fleets of modern times. Japan's initial victories in the Second World War forever destroyed the myth of white supremacy. And if the samurai sword was broken in 1945, nevertheless the slogan of "Asia for the Asiatics" proved to be indestructible. The Japanese wartime policies of freedom and independence for the Asiatic peoples, whether sincere or expedient, would shape the postwar years and the still unknown future.

What next for the world's third strongest economic power?

In 1969, the Japanese-American Assembly, an organization of leading citizens of both countries, agreed that the client-sponsor psychology must be replaced by a new concept of equality. Edwin O. Reischauer, former United States ambassador to Japan, spoke of ending "attitudes developed two decades ago — attitudes conditioned by Japan's defeat and seven years of U.S. occupation."

The Assembly favored the normalization of relations with Communist China, a settlement of the Vietnam War, and a new international climate that would prevent "other Vietnams . . ."

One year later, on November 25, 1970, in Tokyo, an event took place that electrified the Japanese people. It impelled them to question their postwar affluence and to ask the questions a people always ask at a crossroads in their history: "Where are we going? . . . To what future? . . ."

The famous Japanese author Yukio Mishima — founder of a militaristic organization of university students, the Shield Society — accompanied by four of its members, staged a symbolic invasion of the Self-Defense Forces' Headquarters in Tokyo. Mishima, wearing the brown, brass-buttoned Shield uniform, told the astonished officers that the postwar constitution was a sham because it banned the "right" to go to war. Japan, he said, must revive her old values as symbolized in the emperor. When he realized that his passionate harangue had failed to evoke a positive response, Mishima drew his sword and committed the ritual suicide of the samurai, disemboweling himself. One of his aides stepped forward and beheaded Mishima, to be beheaded in turn by the three remaining Shield members.

A macabre ritual, to Westerners, out of Japan's feudal past. A bloody spectacular, almost unbelievable, but it had happened.

To the Japanese, Mishima's sacrifice of his life had another meaning. "The impact of his death on the Japanese people was very great," Professor Takeshi Murumatsu said, and millions of his countrymen would agree with him. "To say the least, it was the greatest psychological shock since World War II."

The ritual suicide and murder, to countless Japanese, was a *kekki* or "righteous uprising" to arouse the nation from its decadence and materialism. Where was the simplicity of olden times? they asked. They recalled the functional, uncluttered houses of their parents and grandparents; the religious purity of Shinto so lacking in elaborate rites and ceremonies; the art that achieved its effects with a minimum of line and color. Too many Japanese worshiped money and pleasure. The rich rode in huge, imported American cars and played golf, the symbol of success. The poor had succumbed to the doctrines of Marx, Lenin, Stalin, and Mao Tse-tung, holding aloft the red banner of Communism instead of the age-old flag of the Rising Sun.

Western materialism and Communism, between them, had cost Japan her very soul.

Mishima and his aide were buried after a Shinto service. Their ideas remained to haunt a nation where millions of Japanese, whether conservative or radical, continue to ask the same disturbing questions: How is man to live in a sick and chaotic world?

The Japanese are a history-minded people. They recalled that three hundred years ago there had been another Mishima — Mito Komon — who had also committed ritual suicide in protest against contacts with the West, limited as these were by the Tokugawa shoguns; he claimed these contacts would rot the foundations of old Japan.

The Shield Society disbanded. But the universities, battlegrounds for years between rightist and leftist students, continue to seethe with discontent. If the Left has found a new god in Karl Marx and his Marxist heirs, the Right upholds the semidivine figure of the emperor.

"Reform the universities," the Left cries. "Throw out the old men! Japan must be Socialist! . . . Communist! . . ." If the Left condemns what they call "merchant values," the Right with equal passion deplores the sacrifice of spiritual values for the sake of economic progress.

Armed with shields and clubs and Molotov cocktails, the student armies battle each other and the police. Their violence surpasses the student violence of the West if only because of its sustained year-in and year-out tenacity and fury.

Yet the Japanese, students as well as all other elements in the population, are the most polite people in the world. The bus conductor will thank you for riding in his bus and invite you to ride again. Everybody, bus conductors and passengers, shop clerks and customers, address each other as *san* or *sama* which means "honored." *Mina Sama* — Honorable Everybody!

The old ways persist. People believe that it is bad luck to leave your chopsticks in a bowl of rice, or to pour hot water into cold. The symbolism is clear. Only a stricken man, never a healthy one, would leave his chopsticks in his bowl. Hot water — the symbol of blood and life — would turn cold as death if mixed with cold water. Japanese mothers delight their children with the exploits of a tiny mannikin — a Japanese Tom Thumb — who only regains his full human size after rescuing the Beautiful Princess. And in the peasant villages, grandmothers frighten their children with tales of the frog-legged Kappa monsters.

The old geography of the Japanese islands, so close to the Asiatic mainland, remains unalterable. For the first fifteen hundred years of Japanese history, Korea was the only foreign land in which the Japanese had an interest. Today, Korea is still vital to Japan (and to China) as a strategic base for a potential enemy. Today, a China no longer weak, but armed with nuclear weapons, challenges the United States in all of Southeast Asia.

The ritualistic suicide of the author Yukio Mishima in November 1970 will be seen by future historians as the first of a series of dramatic events leading to Japan's emergence as an independent power on the world stage.

The second act could be described as a three-ring spectacular. At Peking in April 1971, the American table tennis team in effect lofted a ball over the wall that for twenty years had divided the United States and the People's Republic of China. That same year the Chinese Communists were finally admitted to the United Nations. In February 1972, President Nixon and his entourage of high government officials, journalists, and television commentators flew to China. And the entire world, like some audience at a global circus, sat entranced before their television sets.

There was so much to see. Brilliant Chinese gymnasts and ten-course banquets; the Forbidden City and the Great Wall; and against this backdrop President Nixon meeting with Mao Tse-tung and Chou En-lai.

The Japanese people and their leaders felt a chill of apprehension as they observed the new and unprecedented warmth between the implacable enemies of yesterday. There was the American President at the Great Wall of China, predicting that once the walls of animosity were pierced, the Chinese and American peoples, despite all their differences, could begin to share a peaceful future.

And what about Japan's future? her people asked as they watched the Chinese-American show.

Japanese reaction was almost instantaneous. To safeguard the island empire, new solutions and new friendships had to be created. In the week before President Nixon's departure from Washington, Toyko sent an official mission to North Vietnam. And as the American President spoke at the Great Wall, Tokyo moved closer to the Soviet Union by recognizing the Republic of Outer Mongolia, a state as closely allied to Moscow as Czechoslovakia and Poland.

And the third act? No one can predict the outcome but one thing is clear. Japan will play an increasingly independent role among the players.

"Power comes out of the barrel of a gun," Mao Tse-tung said in one of his famous sayings.

Japan, utterly pacifistic after the Second World War,

still has no army or navy, according to legalistic definitions. But her Self-Defense Forces number 325,000 highly trained men under an elite officer corps that could overnight form the nucleus of a huge and formidable military machine. Why should Japan alone among the world powers surrender the "right" to go to war, if necessary for her security? The Shield Society no longer exists and its founder Yukio Mishima lies buried. But the questions he asked before committing suicide rise like lightning out of his grave.

Ominous questions, but perfectly understandable in a world where the United States, the Soviet Union, the People's Republic of China, Britain, and France all possess nuclear arsenals. And where the three superpowers like chess players with the globe for a table have sat down to a match whose outcome is unpredictable.

Proud of their industrial power, a new nationalism has begun to stir in Japan. And in a divided world, seething with nationalism and racial hatred, the dusty slogans of the Second World War must reverberate, thunderous if still muted, in the minds of many Japanese. And if Japan is still unarmed with the nuclear sword, who can doubt her ability to fashion one?

What will Japan do?

Which side of the Japanese character will prevail? The samurai or the poet?

The first day of every new year is celebrated in Japan as the greatest of all her holidays. It is also *everybody's* birthday — a vast communal celebration. Only the young and completely Westernized Japanese have individual birthdays. By midnight every house is spotless; all debts have been paid; the bells of the temples toll one hundred and eight times, ringing out the old year, ringing in the new. Everybody at midnight goes to the temples and shrines to pray for peace and prosperity; the holiday lasts three days.

Another midnight hour has struck for Japan: a new year, a new destiny.

A new year and destiny, too, for all the great powers.

# Index